Praise for
Bridges to Leadership

Bridges to Leadership is a must-read for every executive. Executives oversee many people, large budgets, tight deadlines, and other headaches. Relieve some stress with quality advice drawn from Oded Agam's thirty-plus years of success in start-ups, multinationals, venture capital, the military, and community service. This book clearly illustrates how to build success with bridges between people.

Tamara Nall | CEO and founder, The Leading Niche

In *Bridges to Leadership*, Oded Agam shares one of the most crucial success factors in life: how to build meaningful, long-lasting bridges between people. By putting the human experience at the center of everything you do, Oded Agam changes the definition of success, no matter what business or life situation applies to you. Success does not come in a vacuum; it happens because of relationships and connections and the way we connect to our peers. This book takes a refreshingly new look at what drives us as human beings. You won't regret reading this book!

Tilmann Gruber | CEO and founder, T'zikal Beauty Group, Inc.

Bridges to Leadership is a truly thoughtful and insightful book. A must-read for entrepreneurs and intrepreneurs who want to become better leaders by effectively building bridges. Whether you are an intrepreneur or entrepreneur leading a start-up, developing a strategy, leading strategic planning, or leading product development for a multinational corporation, we all need to build bridges. Oded shows us how to master it.

Ronald Rubens | CEO and founder, SentioCX

Oded Agam provides invaluable practices to improve your leadership regardless of whether you are a new leader or a well-seasoned executive. His extensive experience across the entire lifecycle of high-tech development and his military and non-profit service allows him to offer real-life examples of how to create value and impact. *Bridges to Leadership* is an excellent window into leading in a global world where relationships are everything.

Lee Ullmann, Ph.D. | senior director global programs, MIT Sloan School of Management

Bridges to Leadership goes beyond an autobiography's usual pat on the back to deliver a well-crafted, understandable story of how to make a project work. Whatever the project, here is a pattern for effective leadership. It's not often that an engineer writes an autobiography that everyone should read, but Oded Agam has done it.

Dr. Kathy Humel | CEO, senior consultant, RX KHumel, LLC

Bridges to Leadership describes how the toughest part of being in charge is making sure the job gets done. Agam's been doing exactly that for thirty-plus years and this is his recipe book for getting it done right. From a small family to a multinational corporation, the rules of good leadership don't change, and Agam's story shows it.

Sanjay Jaybhay | best-selling author of *Invest and Grow Rich*

Oded directly addresses the challenges of high-tech companies. Whether start-ups or multinationals, those challenges can be huge, but simple steps make the impossible attainable. See thirty-plus years of experience and a lifetime of learning in a fascinating, readable story that can help you get all the pieces of the puzzle into place.

Shawn Johal | business growth coach, Elevation Leaders, Bestselling Author of *The Happy Leader*

BRIDGES *to* LEADERSHIP

VISION, EMPOWERMENT
STRATEGY, PEOPLE, ACTION

ODED AGAM

Leaders
Press

Leaders
Press

Copyright © 2024 Oded Agam
Published in the United States by Leaders Press.
www.leaderspress.com

ISBN **978-1-63735-290-8** (hcv)
ISBN **978-1-63735-167-3** (pbk)
ISBN **978-1-63735-168-0** (ebook)

Library of Congress Control Number: **2022906090**

To my mom and my dad,
my teachers, my role models, my inspiration.
I love you with all my heart.
Thank you for everything.

To my wife,
my soulmate, my partner, my best friend.
You are the love of my life.
Thank you for everything.

Contents

Introduction 1

Chapter 1: Start-ups in Israel 13

Chapter 2: Coming to America 37

Chapter 3: Creating Your Own Start-up 59

Chapter 4: The Multinational Corporation Way 69

Chapter 5: An "Atomic" Education 87

Chapter 6: Reaching for the Skylake 99

Chapter 7: A Strategic Outlook Leads Disruptive
Innovation 119

Chapter 8: Process Makes for Progress 143

Chapter 9: The Military 151

Chapter 10: Nonprofits 163

Chapter 11: Venture Capital 181

Chapter 12: Leadership 213

Words Before We Part 233

About Oded Agam 237

Introduction

I Am a Bridge

When I meet people and introduce myself, I tell them "I'm a bridge."

They typically ask, "What do you mean?"

I answer, "I build bridges."

Then they inquire, "Can you be more specific?"

I continue, "I build bridges between the past and the present; between the present and the future; between technology and business; between what is needed or desired and what is possible or available; between people from different disciplines and cultures."

Not too many really get me right away. They may say, "Businesses exist solely to make profit for their stockholders, not their stakeholders. How, then, does bridge building profit the stockholders?"

A very good question, to which I answer, "In a free, capitalist society, a business needs to create value for all of its stakeholders in order to maximize value for its stockholders."

I take the multidisciplinary approach to innovation: bridge the gap between people and ideas with technologies from different specialties, then combine them in novel ways. You can then address needs, overcome challenges, solve problems, create solutions, and satisfy desires in astoundingly successful ways.

Gaps are the natural result of the differences among people. Stockholders, employees, customers, and others have different specific goals for a business. Bridge the gaps among them, and you've minimized the gaps between expectation and outcome, which could be a very good definition of success. Success makes people happy, and at the end of the day, if creating my success helps create your success, we both make a profit, even if our definitions of "profit" differ, for example:

❖ The employees profit by enjoying being at work, advancing their career, and having an impact; they get promotions, pay raises, added professional training, and better professional reputation, and they are motivated to show creativity, innovate, and go the extra mile.

❖ Management profits by increasing their span of control and their impact, getting bonuses, stock options, awards, and other recognitions, and their professional reputations grow.

❖ Stockholders profit by getting increased dividends and higher return on their investment, and their judgment (in choosing the company and hiring the management) is justified, therefore, improving their professional reputation.

❖ Customers and users profit by getting a product or a service that better solves their problems, fulfills their aspirations, and brings joy to their lives, or in some cases, improves their quality of life and life span, more efficiently, more reliably, or more cost-effectively.

I would like to profit, and I'm sure you do as well, so I help you build these bridges so we can all profit.

For Whom Is This Book Written?

This book is primarily for high-tech or finance executives, whether in an established multinational conglomerate, an investment firm, or a brand-new start-up. I hope to make clear to you how to dream and then make that dream a reality.

That said, the principles and methods discussed have application in almost any organization. Good leadership in a high-tech start-up is good leadership in a century-old charity. If you're smart enough to be studying leadership and reading this book, then you're smart enough to recognize ideas and concepts that'll be of value to your particular situation.

For the last thirty-plus years, I've worked in and around high tech. Some of those years found me leading corporate strategic planning for winning products that generated multibillion-dollar profits. Other years found me leading innovative high-tech start-ups solving big problems or investing in high-tech start-ups generating healthy returns for investors.

During all those years, people kept telling me, "Money makes the world go round."

No, absolutely not! That is a false statement of the cruelest, most injurious kind—the kind that inevitably leads people to failure! My experience has taught me a far different axiom:

People make the world go round.

Companies don't succeed, products don't succeed, marketing campaigns don't succeed—people succeed! If people don't succeed, no value is created.

This is a book about people: how people lead other people to deliver value to people. This is the essence of vision, strategy, entrepreneurship, innovation, and leadership all rolled into one simple maxim.

If you create and capture value, then everybody is happy, except, perhaps, your competitors, and is that not as it should be?

"Retrospection" is the measuring and analyzing of past events or experiences. It's a critical element in my story, and in everything else in life. You may think of this book as a midway retrospective of my career and life so far. Hopefully, through it, you'll come to understand the effects of what I've done in building bridges and be ready to generate similar effects for yourself and your organization.

I'm not done yet. I am only at the middle of my life journey, and there's more to come—more to learn, more to experience, more to do, more to accomplish, more to teach, more to appreciate, more to enjoy. This book is for people who are at the start or in the middle of their career, looking to grow, improve, learn, and become even more successful than they already are.

Before we start, a note of caution and an apology if I seem repetitive: If the reader is to get the full value of this narrative, it's vital that the reader internalize my perspective. This is a story about people. It's not about technology, marketing, sales, finance—any of that. We will discuss, at length, what we did, but the point of the story is the individuals who did it—people who got together to bring value to people.

I owe my thanks to the many who were part of this exciting journey—a few are mentioned here, most are not. I apologize in advance for those not given the public acknowledgment they're due. All of you are cherished in my mind and heart, and all of you have a part in the successful creation and delivery of value for people by people.

Enjoy!

Who Am I?

I am a high-tech engineer turned business executive turned investor. Here's a brief summary of my professional career since I graduated from the Technion—Israel Institute of Technology—in March 1990:

- ❖ Five years in the Israeli Navy as a technical officer
- ❖ Eleven years in start-ups leading R&D, business, marketing and product management
- ❖ Eleven years in Intel doing strategic planning and product definition
- ❖ Six years in venture capital
- ❖ Nine years (volunteer) on the executive board of a nonprofit-association—Big Brothers Big Sisters of Israel (the last six as chairman of the executive board)
- ❖ Twenty years (volunteer) as a leader of the NYU Alumni Club of Israel (the last nine years as club president)

Above all other roles and achievements, I am a husband, happily married to Anat, my wife, for more than thirty years, whom I love so much, and a proud dad to three exceptional children—Amit, Neta, and Edo—who are already mature young adults making their way in our world. I love them deeply and enjoy watching their journey.

The Early Years

I actually began that resume at age fourteen, when I decided I didn't want to attend high school in my hometown of Ra'ananna, as all my friends would. Instead, I spent an hour twice daily going to the Handasaim High School, also called the Tel Aviv University Secondary School.

This is a special high school, established in 1962 as part of Tel Aviv University. At that time, it was located right next to that campus in a quiet Tel Aviv neighborhood called Ramat Aviv. (It moved in 2005, long after I graduated, to the city of Herzliya.) Handasaim High School focuses on technology and science. Its mission is to educate and nurture the next generation of scientists and engineers for Israel. This is a high school that takes only the best and brightest of children from across the Tel Aviv metropolitan area and the suburbs. The forty students in my class—four girls and thirty-six boys—studied and practiced many aspects of technology, such as electrical engineering, computer science, mechanical engineering, industrial engineering, and more.

I probably decided on this course because of my dad. I call myself a second-generation high-tech person. My dad worked in the high-tech sector before it was even called "high-tech." His was the world of economics and finance. He worked as chief financial officer and controller for large Israeli companies in both the public and private sectors, especially science-based industries, including CDC (Control Data Corporation), 4-D Software, Metatron, Pioneer Concrete, Beged Or, Nilit, and others. He later started a private practice where for more than twenty years, he provided local and overseas firms with specialized financial consulting services. His client base included Israeli companies in technology and American companies that do business with Israel.

Through my dad, I absorbed the high-tech feeling and thinking from a very young age. We were always the first family among our friends to have the latest and greatest electronics and computers. I remember, for example, 19 November 1977, when Anwar Sadat, then-president of Egypt, became the first Arab leader to visit Israel officially. My parents invited all of their friends to our home to watch Sadat's arrival at Ben-Gurion Airport on our color TV. Everybody else around us had only black-and-white TVs at the time. It was a big celebration for all of us, and we could literally see the winds of peace arriving—a very optimistic day.

I also remember being impressed when during Purim (an annual Jewish celebration), my parents went to a party for the employees of CDC (back then, a world leader among computing companies), and my dad wore a costume that looked like a mainframe computer, created by my mom.

Mom also had a significant influence over me. She is a veteran educator who taught art education to thousands of kindergarten and elementary school teachers at Beit Berl College and Levinsky College of Education.

Sometimes I think that I inherited my left brain from my dad and my right brain from my mom. My dad gave me the ability to relate to mathematics, facts, logic, and linear thinking. My mom gave me the ability to imagine, visualize, and think holistically. I bless, cherish, and thank them both—they are so important to me, and I love them so much.

During the writing of this book, my dad's health deteriorated, and he passed away at age eighty-seven.

He had a full life and left a great legacy for our family, and a big hole in our hearts. Some of him is embedded in me, and I will continue to love him as my hero for the rest of my life.

Beginnings of My Practical Education

An important memory that shaped my teenage thinking came in the late '70s and early '80s. My dad won some achievement award at work, and he received a prize—a trip to the Bahamas to participate in the CDC global sales conference. When he came back home, he had many stories about the conference and the islands and brought me one of these famous Bahamian colorful shirts. This was one of my first lessons on corporate America:

To get the most out of people, it is important to recognize and reward them in a meaningful way—beyond money—one that would be seen by others and appreciated by the person rewarded.

Thanks to Dad, we had our first gaming console (an Atari) in the late '70s and our first home computer in the early '80s, (an IBM Personal Computer). Thanks to my Atari system, our home became the mecca of gaming for many of my friends. I remember spending many hours enjoying these games with friends. Here began my exploration of the computer world. By age fourteen, it was clear to me that I want to spend the rest of my life doing something in the technology world. That led me to study at Handasaim.

Although it was a one-hour drive (each way) from Ra'ananna to Tel Aviv, I enjoyed this time. Each morning, my dad drove me to school on the way to his office in Tel Aviv. It was a guaranteed hour of quality time with

Dad every day. Afternoons saw me homeward bound on a bus with friends also attending the high school. During that first year, I experienced a huge change in my thinking about myself as I related to others around me. Before Handasaim, I was always among the top three students in class, but my Handasaim class had over three dozen students, all as smart as me and some definitely smarter. Some became lifelong friends.

During my youth, apart from school, I spent a lot of time with the Scouts. This was my social scene, and again, the many friendships I made there continue to this day. I recommend very strongly that all teenagers join the Scouts or some other youth organization and take part in all that the organization does. The experiences I had shaped much of who I am as a person and leader. Those activities helped form my personality and brought me great leadership and social skills, and if you really get actively involved in your group, it can do that for you as well.

America—My First Bridge

At sixteen years old, our family relocated to Brookline, Massachusetts, a suburb of Boston, where my mom studied for her master's degree in art education at the Massachusetts College of Art & Design. I attended Brookline High School for my sophomore year. This was actually my second time living in the US. The first began at age eighteen months and ended at age three and a half. We lived in New York City, and my parents say that when we returned to Israel, I spoke English with a perfect American accent—the English of a three-year-old. Both shaped my understanding of Americans and their culture.

One early lesson involved American-style marketing: We were sitting in our American literature class when someone knocked on the door. The teacher let in a man dressed as a clown and holding a bouquet of colorful balloons. He went directly to a girl in the class and handed her the balloons, telling her this was from her boyfriend—who was sitting next to her—then sang a happy birthday song to her. That day, I learned that you can do amazing stuff in marketing, but take note:

You have to make sure other people see what you do in order to make a lasting impression that inspires people.

Studying in an American public high school provided me with many typical experiences that American teenagers have, which has helped me to "dress up as an American" during later phases of life. I'll never be a true American, but I do my best to behave like one (and relate to Americans) in certain situations.

During our time in the USA, I also learned about the importance of family and flexibility. My parents were always "citizens of the world." They cherished openness and freedom, their families, and equal opportunity for both of them. When Mom decided to get her master's degree, there was no program in her domain of expertise in any Israeli university, so Dad made it possible for her and me and my siblings to live in Massachusetts while he continued his employment in Israel.

How did they balance these two conflicting goals?

They built a bridge: My mom, siblings, and I moved to Brookline while my dad stayed in Israel. Every two or three weeks, he came over to Brookline for a week to ten days. During holidays and summer break, we flew to Israel to spend time with Dad. As Mom had to continue her studies after we returned to Israel, she returned to the USA for another semester while the kids stayed with Dad in Israel. Before returning to the USA, she cooked for several days, leaving us a freezer filled with home-cooked meals that lasted for several weeks. Mom completed the last of her studies remotely, graduating with her MA in art education.

I didn't fully understand it at the time, but this was my first lesson in bridge building. Life-changing experiences usually follow a simple pattern:

- ❖ Here is the problem.
- ❖ Here are some potential solutions.
- ❖ Here is the solution we tried.
- ❖ Here is the profit.

In this case, it looks like this:

- ❖ The problem: Mom studying in USA; Dad working in Israel.
- ❖ The potential solutions: one of them giving up on their dreams or getting a divorce.
- ❖ The solution we tried: hybrid living in both countries.
- ❖ The profit: Mom completed her MA; Dad kept his job; the kids spent time with both; I learned a pattern for success.

My parents were great role models for me, as they were formulating creative solutions that considered each of their and our needs. They maintained the bridge that existed among members of our family by paying attention to the needs of each member. They also bridged the gap between their professional and personal lives by addressing their individual needs in the context of the family's needs.

Military Service

During my junior year at high school back in Israel, I made my second life-changing decision. At seventeen, I decided to join the Atuda, the Academic Reserves of Tzahal, the Israel Defense Forces (IDF). Israel requires military service from every citizen, beginning at age eighteen. As part of the Atuda, I would attend university first, get a degree, then serve active duty in the IDF as an officer. I applied to the Technion and the Atuda and was accepted by both. During Technion's summer break, I attended the IDF Officers Academy and graduated successfully. Four years later, with my bachelor of science in electrical engineering, I began five years' service in the Israeli Navy as a program officer and systems engineer with the rank of lieutenant. I completed that service and was honorably discharged as a captain.

Now, with great training and solid work experience, I felt ready to begin the next phase of my professional journey—high-tech start-ups.

Chapter 1

⚜

Start-ups in Israel

Why Israeli Start-ups Are Successful

Israel, due to its geographical position and the heritage of the Jewish people, is uniquely situated as fertile ground for starting businesses. Many people, in most countries, feel the need to gain experience in a large corporation where they have a steady paycheck, professional mentoring, a sponsor to attend relevant trade shows, and a support staff (HR, accountants, and lawyers—all paid by someone else) so that they can focus on gaining experience without having to do everything on their own.

In Israel, the attitude differs. Because Israeli culture was, and still is, in itself, a school for entrepreneurs, so many young adults work in start-ups. Growing up as part of that culture, I felt comfortable jumping into the challenges of the start-up sector.

What, specifically, in Israeli culture gave me that confidence?

If you live in New York City, or any place with a significant Jewish population, you've probably heard the word *chutzpah*. Chutzpah is about setting audacious goals and achieving them even if the odds of success seem slim in the beginning. Chutzpah is often required to create a bridge between the reality of the present and the potential of the future, a bridge between the impossible and the possible. It's about having the grit to continue fighting for your cause and achieving your goals no matter how hard the journey is. It is about challenging the status quo and always asking "Why?" Chutzpah takes nothing for granted.

There's a lot of chutzpah in Israel. We typically like to choose our own way of living. Many Israelis don't take "no" for an answer, and they realize that sometimes it's better to ask for forgiveness than permission while accepting the appropriate cautionary footnote: Sometimes there's no forgiveness to be had, so choose carefully!

In short, we take chances because we're good at beating the odds, or at least, we think we are. Non-Israelis sometimes think that Israelis are rude or rough, but we see it differently. We know what we want, and we go for it. Our culture is one of tenacity, and we're willing to do what it takes. Many times, we don't have a choice; we just have to do it to survive.

That's why Israel has long been known as the "Start-up Nation." Israel is home to over six thousand active start-ups, making it the world leader for start-ups per capita.[1] In fact, there's an increasing number of "unicorns"—private companies worth more than $1 billion—founded by Israelis as well as an increase in research and development (R&D) centers of multinational corporations (MNCs) operating in Israel—over five

[1] Idan Adler, "The Israeli Technological Eco-System," Deloitte Israel (Deloitte Touche Tohmatsu Limited, January 16, 2016), https://www2.deloitte.com/il/en/pages/innovation/article/the_israeli_technological_eco-system.html.

hundred at the time this book was written. Israel, one might say, is transforming into the "Scale-Up Nation."[2]

What secrets make a tiny country of only nine million home to so many successful high-tech companies?

Well, in my opinion, it's all about the people and the location. Innovation and entrepreneurship are necessities. There's no other way. You must innovate and create—you have to have some *chutzpah*—to survive and thrive.

Through investing in Israeli high-tech, leading corporate groups, start-up companies, and organizations based in Israel, I've encountered many Israelis who have several characteristics that make them innovative and entrepreneurial. Others can learn from these qualities:

Adopt a Global Mindset

Although Israel isn't geographically an island, our state has many characteristics of an island. On the west, the Mediterranean Sea borders us. On all other sides, we border countries that don't have democratic, free-market economies, nor do they share other key cultural factors. In fact, the distance between Israel and another OECD country is more than five hundred miles, with air or sea transport being the only options.[3] This means that any business (start-up or large corporation) that aspires to succeed must think on a global scale from day one. The market is just too small to enable a big economic success

---

[2] Eliyahu Korn and Ayelet Slasky, "10 Israeli-Founded Companies Reach Unicorn Status in 1st Quarter of 2021," NoCamels (NoCamels, April 15, 2021), https://nocamels.com/2021/04/9-israeli-companies-unicorn-1b-q1-2021/.

[3] OECD: The Organisation for Economic Co-operation and Development–a multinational association currently comprising 38 member nations–was founded in 1961 to stimulate economic progress and world trade.

if one doesn't also trade and engage with the rest of the world from the get-go.

Be Resourceful

I've observed that "islanders" typically develop a set of survival characteristics that allow them to flourish in a remote area. They often have limited resources at hand and must be imaginative. They must find novel ways of doing things and do those things in an optimized manner. This is especially important for start-ups, most of which beginning with limited resources and must find creative ways to expand their business.

Here are two brief examples:

MaxPO Home Networks, a start-up I co-founded, had very limited resources in the beginning, and we couldn't afford to hire all the full-time experts we wanted. Therefore, we the founders had to do a lot of the work ourselves, hiring part-time sub-contractors to augment us and do the things too difficult for us to complete on our own. In order to develop our first prototype, we had to wear many hats:

- ❖ We, the founding partners, did the market research.
- ❖ We identified customer needs.
- ❖ We developed product requirements, software architecture, the actual code, the quality assurance plan, and the go-to-market strategy.
- ❖ We worked with the design partners—the future potential customers and users.
- ❖ We did all this while also doing the administrative things needed to run the business.

We had to do this at record speed and with very little money. This enabled us to raise money from angel investors and get a grant from the Israeli Innovation Authority. We could then make further progress and make our solution ready for engagement with our target market companies, like Comcast in the USA.

While at Intel, different engineering groups sometimes competed for the same project. I've seen Israeli engineering group managers take proactive and imaginative action to ensure their group received the responsibility to complete a project. Once, I watched an Israeli manager go to the Intel headquarters and walk the corridor next to the room where a decision meeting about a certain project was taking place. That manager hoped that during the break, the participants would go out into the corridor and "stumble" onto him, bringing that team to the top of the decision-makers' minds and making sure they were selected to lead that very lucrative project. And that is exactly what happened—they got the project.

Prioritize Diversity

The "Jewish People" are a very diverse group. Israel is a melting pot for Jewish immigrants from around the globe. The Bible as well as other archeological findings tell us that the ancient Jewish people were exiled from Israel to Egypt, Iran, Iraq, and other Middle Eastern nations. About two thousand years ago, Jewish people immigrated to Greece, Italy, Spain, and other parts of Western Europe. In the centuries since, Jews emigrated to Eastern Europe and Northern Africa, eventually spreading us among the Americas, Russia, even the Far East and Australia.

In the second half of the nineteenth century, immigration patterns changed. Jewish immigrants started to gather to Israel rather than spread out, and these waves of immigration intensified in the first half of the twentieth century. This brought together Jewish people who'd lived in Arab countries (the "Sephardic" Jews) and others who'd lived in Western European countries (the "Ashkenazi" Jews).

World War II and the Holocaust formed a major inflection point of Jewish history. Millions were slaughtered, and others were forced to leave Europe. This resulted in the establishment of the State of Israel in 1948. Since then, many Jews have made *aliya* (Hebrew: "going up"), meaning they relocated to the new (but old) homeland, as Theodor Herzl, the founder of political Zionism—known as "The Prophet of the State"—called it in his 1902 book *Altneuland*.

These waves of immigrants from all parts of the world create an extremely diverse society. This has been a huge blessing to Israel, as the different mindsets of people foster creativity and innovation. For example, as the Soviet Union broke up in the 1990s, a new wave of Russian-speaking Jewish immigrants (mostly from Russia and Ukraine) came to Israel. Many of these were experienced technology workers and provided a big boost to Israel's high-tech sector.

In addition, about one-fifth of the population of Israel are Arabs—both Muslim and Christian. Although they're a minority, they are represented in many places including the *Knesset* (Israel's parliament), the healthcare system, and, to a growing extent, in academia and industry.

Israel is diverse in other matters as well. For example, many have observed that Tel Aviv is especially friendly to the LGBTQ+ community. Furthermore, Israel has the fourth highest number of vegans per capita, roughly 5 percent of the population. These and other factors combine to create a population with wide-ranging experiences and hopes.

As I said earlier, gaps are a natural characteristic of human societies, and bridges cross these gaps. Each employee brings their own skills and mindset, their way of thinking and doing things, based on their culture and experience. Connecting them in a nonjudgmental manner, where any ideas can be put on the table for discussion, creates synergy.

Synergy means the whole is greater than the sum of the parts. The best-known example is the Belgian draft horse—once society's favored transportation option. One good Belgian can pull about eight thousand pounds (twice its own weight) in cart and cargo, but two, working together, can pull about twenty-four thousand pounds— six times the weight of each horse!

A diverse workforce brings together distinct viewpoints that can combine into novel approaches to problems, allowing you to better serve your users, customers, and partners.

You can also get a better understanding of your target markets. For example, when I was involved in the definition of Intel's system-on-chip for mobile devices, we had members on our team from Africa. They told us that many mobile phones in Africa were secondhand— first used in the West for some years, then refurbished and sold in Africa for a second life. Why is this important? This previously unknown fact redefined the product lifespan, which impacted specifications for reliability, durability, and other aspects of the product. If we didn't have team members who'd grown up on other continents, we might never have learned this key fact, and we might've created a less valuable product.

Learn and Adapt

All immigrants, regardless of origin or destination, have something in common: They're forced to adapt in order to thrive in their new society. Many must learn a new language; they encounter new customs or a new climate. Sometimes they even adopt new names. Success demands adaptation to the new environment and new norms—to a point. What is very successful in "the Old Country" may not lead to success in the new.

High-tech companies operate in a dynamic ecosystem that keeps changing exponentially, making it critical for them to evolve, adapt, and change to fit the ever-changing world. The "world of tomorrow" can literally be one day away. Be ready for it! Or better yet, take actions to bridge the future and the present.

Take Risks to Overcome Obstacles

In general, I've observed that Israelis don't buy much into the concept of "impossible." If you want to get Israelis to do something difficult, challenge them by saying something like, "Oh, I don't think you can make that happen." Again, it's chutzpah. We set audacious goals and find ways to accomplish them. I think Israelis live by that old proverb, "Everything is impossible...until someone does it."

Ask Why

In most places around the globe, leadership is hierarchal. When a manager asks an employee to do something, he or she will do it or at least try their best. Israel is different. When you ask Israelis to do something, especially in a start-up, they will first ask, "Why?" Israelis like to understand the why and not just the what. They want to challenge you and make sure that there is a good reason for doing what you ask them to do.

In my experience, when people understand the why, they'll do a better job because they better understand the problem they're trying to solve and the importance of solving it.

Verify Execution

In the Israel Defense Forces officers, as in every military, so far as I know, are responsible to get the job done. Officers need to train their people, trust them, delegate, and empower them to get the job done, but in the end, the officer is responsible for completion of the task. Israelis understand that authority, responsibility, and accountability are interchangeable. We may pass the football; we don't pass the buck.

Be Friendly

Israelis are often very direct in their approach, and this sometimes requires adjustment for non-Israelis at first. However, this direct approach is not meant to be unsociable or inhospitable. Most Israelis have a very friendly nature, in my experience. We look to foster strong, long-term relationships with customers, partners, investors, and employees, but we don't have time to waste.

Among all the assets Israel has, human capital is the most important, and we've come to feel that wasting time talking around subjects instead of getting directly to the point of a discussion wastes that precious resource.

How Start-ups Are Successful

Research and Development Is Fundamental

A couple of months prior to my discharge (after five years' service in the Israeli Navy), I started looking for my next chapter in life. My path toward high tech was clear, and I pondered over some strategic choices: Should I join a big corporation or a start-up? What role did I want—research and development or sales and marketing? Should I start my own business? Should I focus on defense systems, where I had experience, or some new area?

The last question was the easiest. After five years working on weapon systems, I wanted something different. I wanted a role in a civilian industry where I can make the world a better place, contribute to the well-being of people, solve problems, fulfill needs, and build bridges.

The other questions were more difficult to answer, so I discussed my options with many people whose opinions and perspective I valued. First and foremost, I talked extensively with my wife, Anat. She has an incredible feel for the right thing to do or say in every situation—woman's intuition, maybe. I truly value her opinion on everything and consult with her as much as possible.

I also spoke to my parents and siblings. They taught me the importance of the family from a very young age. I remember that while I was at Intel, I participated in a leadership development course that included work on understanding the key values that drive us. For me, family has always been top of the list.

After all this discussion, I concluded that five years in a "big org" environment was enough for now. I'd like to join a high-tech start-up. I felt it was too early for me to become an entrepreneur and initiate my own start-up, alone or with co-founders. However, I did want a smaller organization with more freedom to operate and less defined boundaries where people expect you to think big and bold.

This decision came after weeks of research, not about products of my potential employers, but about me and my direction in life. My job search began, one might say, with an extensive research program—what did I want, and where could I get it? Every successful venture that I'm aware of, both corporate and personal, begins with that same research. The more you do, the more knowledge you have about all aspects of the problem at hand and the better chance you have to create an effective solution.

So in that pre-internet era, I found a newspaper ad for a systems engineer at a start-up called RADCOM. I'm not sure what attracted my eyes, but I contacted them, and after two interviews, it became clear to both sides that it was a perfect match. I quickly received an offer letter, signed it, and started working there a few days after leaving the navy.

Making Big Decisions

Having done the research and armed with the facts after exploring how to determine what path to take in my career or move elsewhere, I was lucky enough to get a very different, but very complementary, advice from my dad and mom:

My dad, an economist, taught me to look at decisions from the economic value perspective. He taught me analytical thinking. My dad always optimized for economic value—that is, earn more money and pay less in expenses.

My mom taught me to look at decisions from the quality-of-life perspective. She taught me to consider what would lead to greater happiness, both in the short and long term. She always balanced choices by looking at two main questions—happiness and time.

I learned to combine their thinking and consider three things—economics, happiness, and time. To minimize the amount of time and money it takes to get to the highest economic value in order to maintain the highest happiness level for the longest time. (It sounds like a simple equation, but it can be difficult to implement.)

To satisfy both methods presented by my parents, you must first determine the endgame scenario: what does the world look like and feel like when you've won or succeeded? Figure this out, and it becomes easier to determine the right steps to reach the point of success.

You are effectively building a bridge between where you are and where you'd like to be in five years, ten years, or more. You determine questions, consult with others, then take all the information you have and make choices; each of which becomes a metaphorical girder in this figurative structure. Once on the path, you'll see that adjustments will be needed, so keep one eye on the horizon and one ear to the ground, and adjust as needed. Remember the military cliché?

No battle plan ever survives first contact with the enemy.

Build the Bridge

RADCOM hired me to ensure testability and quality of the product we developed (a highly sophisticated communication network testing solution) to enable a smooth transfer of the product from R&D to the production department. As I did this, it quickly became apparent that there were bugs and inefficiencies in the seams between hardware and software development of the unit. It was also clear from the beginning that these two departments were very different. Each department naturally attracts a different type of engineer with, obviously, very different skill sets but also very different mindsets, creating a lot of potential for conflict. These bugs and inefficiencies resulted in frequent problems that took a lot of time to fix. The departments didn't know any of this because they weren't talking to each other.

The problems were not only within the R&D department, but they also involved other departments as well. R&D engineers thought their responsibility lay completely in developing the product, but production needed tools to complete quality control testing on the product during the manufacturing process. R&D thought that production would develop those tools, but production didn't have the right people to do that, nor did they have the intimate knowledge of the system to let them do it.

"What we have here is a failure to communicate," says the famous movie quote.[4]

The solution, obviously, was to bridge this gap. I set out with a two-fold strategy:

❖ **Meetings**, including all stakeholders, needed to be conducted regularly, where problems were raised and solutions proposed with clear next steps for resolution. Sometimes it was whole teams, sometimes team leads, sometimes specific team members, depending on the goals for that meeting. Typically, meetings were weekly, but many daily or even twice-daily meetings were held, depending on the urgency and what was required to identify and resolve issues.
❖ **Documentation** of systems and processes in a clear way got everybody on the same page, reducing the possibility of misunderstandings.

After holding the meetings and reviewing the documentation, it became clear that R&D was the place to develop quality-control tools and functionality-testing methods to be used during production.

This improved communication created an integrated development process that resulted in simpler, faster transfer from research to development to production. It also shortened production time and increased quality.

I should stress that there was never a question of team rivalry. The teams worked together and respected each other. The core problem was lack of understanding of the other team's mindset and way of doing things. However, in some of these conflicts, interests beyond

---

[4] *Cool Hand Luke* (Jalem Productions/Warner Brothers, 1967).

the business and the technology were involved. I saw some people very adamant about having it their way to prove they were right and others wrong. Part of building bridges is often crafting compromises that sometimes meant some parties were not fully satisfied. I found that when everybody was equally dissatisfied, I'd chosen the right way to go—the best compromise for the company.

These meetings and the documentation also made it clear that on some issues, we didn't have the tools we needed for success. We lacked tools to do quality assurance (QA) of the hardware design, so I developed tools and methodologies for that QA.

For example, I drove the use of JTAG (Joint Test Action Group, an industry-standard for testing printed circuit boards) in the company, making us, I think, one of the first Israeli companies to use that protocol in the mid-1990s. I also hired developers to create software that tested the functionality of the hardware. One in particular, Eyal Nir, who remains a close friend to this day, was hired specifically because he was older and more experienced than me. In this, I followed a basic business leadership maxim:

Hire the best people for the job, especially if they're smarter and better at the task than you.

All this created a more holistic collaboration framework, allowing the teams to work together more effectively toward reaching their common goal.

I didn't have specific orders to do this, but I was responsible for testability, quality, and transfer to production. I realized that in order to do my job effectively, I had to reengineer RADCOM's way of doing business to ensure they helped each other identify and fix the problems. This ensured that the company provided the required value to customers and end-users.

One might think the need for this sort of bridge was obvious, and people would just do it naturally. In truth, it doesn't just happen. People get wrapped up in their own responsibilities and often don't understand the problems faced by others. These bridges must be built intentionally to connect people and ensure they talk with each other, understand each other, help each other, and drive the whole product through every stage, from initial concept to end-user delivery in the shortest possible time and using the minimum of resources.

Now, cynics may say, "Meetings are where minutes are taken and hours are lost." Absolutely correct if you don't do it right! Meetings facilitated by skilled and experienced leaders are productive and effective. Effective meetings comprise three stages:

1. Pre-Meeting

The leader must establish the goal of the meeting, the correct participants, and what each should bring to the meeting and convey it all clearly to all participants prior to the meeting.

I like a methodology called management by presentation (MBP). The leader must be clear as to who needs to present and what material they will present, then invite them to do so. The leader may also host prep meetings with the presenters (privately) to ensure they bring the right content and present it in a clear, meaningful way. It's also important to allocate enough time for each presenter as well as the questions and answers section, if and when applicable.

2. Meeting

The leader needs to start on time, not waiting for those who come late. Do this once or twice, and people will start arriving on time. If many people are chronically late, use this trick: Set and start the meeting at 10:15 a.m. (instead of 10:00 a.m.). People are more likely to be on time when the starting time of the meeting is not a round hour. Review the agenda, focus, and goal. Consider the presenters and allocated time and the decisions to be made. Then give them their allocated time to present their material. During presentations, identify and assign the action items, owners of each, and schedules of completion. Review these at the end of the meeting.

3. Post-Meeting

Even the best leaders sometime forget this, but I find it the most important step: Shortly after the meeting—timing is important as you don't want to lose momentum and you always want to portray a sense of urgency and control of the process—the leader publishes the minutes to all participants and others with a need to know.

In my mind, meeting minutes are neither a burden nor an afterthought. They should be written by the leader, not a junior person or a secretary/admin. The minutes are a significant tool in the hands of the leader to drive action through the organization—and beyond, if the meeting included external people. The minutes drive action as part of the relationship with those people and their organizations. Here are my must-have sections of the minutes:

- ❖ **Participants**. These might just be first names, might be full names, might include title and organization as well, depending on who was involved. (If you find yourself in a situation where you talk with people about the meeting, it's always better to know if they participated or not.)

❖ **Precis**. This is a bullet list with succinct, precise sentences that describe the key points presented or discussed in the meeting. The shorter the better, without losing content or meaning.

❖ **Proceedings**. This is a summary of all major points of discussion. If presentations were made, graphics, files, links, and other resources can be attached. Don't repeat the presentations. It's redundant. People will likely not read them and will not take them seriously. Note: The difficulty and cost of an audio-video copy has dropped so low that most organizations can afford a complete recording of all important meetings. For legal reasons, these can be valuable. Of course, each situation is different, each organization must decide how far they need to go, but this can be a case where more is truly better than less. Access to such recordings (again, for legal reasons) probably should be limited to those with a need to know. Nevertheless, even when such a recording exists, it is still important to write and send the minutes of the meeting to save time for people. A typical one-hour meeting can be summarized in minutes that can be read in only a few minutes.

❖ **Decisions and action items (AIs, or as they are called at Intel, ARs, or action required)**. After the discussion points, list the decisions, who owns them, and (sometimes but this isn't always the best plan) the expected completion dates.

❖ **Highlights**. Mark in yellow the top takeaways from the meeting. This should never be more than 25 to 30 percent of the text—key questions, key decisions, key AIs. Make it enough that anyone in a hurry could read just the highlighted text and get the gist of what happened.

Minutes are important. They convey thoughts, discussions, ideas, and decisions. So spend the time and get them right. Minutes are the most effective way to disseminate communication across the organization internally and an effective way to align and manage expectations with external organizations—customers, partners, service providers, subcontractors, and others.

Through all this at RADCOM, I developed testing procedures and wrote detailed explanations to production on what, why, and how they should test, benchmarks and success criteria, and more. I had all sides review these documents and provide feedback until (after a few iterations) we reached consensus on documents that clearly outlined the methodology of transferring products from R&D to production and how the products should be QA'd before shipment to customers.

This process occupied several months, and at the end of it, we had a significant increase in productivity, effectiveness, and quality of the products being shipped to customers. By that time, most of the people in the company knew me. I was being noticed and respected, and my voice was heard and appreciated. I had made a big impact on the direction of the company.

Nobody told me to do what I did. I just knew it was the right thing to do, and I went ahead, did it, convinced people to help me, and made it work. This is probably the first time I realized the most important idea for a successful leader: "Always think like the CEO."

It doesn't matter if you're part of a small or large organization or your role in it. You're always better off if you think with the "bird's-eye view" of the whole organization. Many times, we get caught up in the narrow view, thinking about the benefit to our own team, our own department, and our own project. That's a bad plan. Only when you consider the big picture, as the CEO must, can you see the holistic view, the benefits to the entire company of the work you and your teammates do, and what's needed to obtain those benefits. This will ensure you will be noticed by top executives, and soon enough, you may become one of those top executives.

Analysis Paralysis or Just Do It

I've seen people debating what and how to do things but hesitating to start doing because they are not sure of all the steps on the way to get where they'd like to be. This is analysis paralysis, where they keep analyzing potential paths forever and never get the job done. At such times, I tell them an old story:

A mathematician and an engineer stand in the doorway to a large room. In the far corner sits a beautiful chocolate cake, ready to eat. They are told they can move towards the cake, but each time they move, they can only move half-way to the cake. The mathematician walks away because, mathematically, he will never get to the cake. The engineer immediately starts walking across the room...

The story is ridiculous—both people would know that, eventually, they'd be close enough to reach out and pick up the cake. But expand the story's idea to real-world problems. You're in a new position or working on a new project:

❖ You don't know every possible fact or outcome. Every project faces challenges unforeseen at the outset. I repeat the old military proverb, "No battle plan ever survives first contact with the enemy." So you must be ready to adapt.
❖ You may "know" some facts that are incorrect, especially if you're working on something innovative. How old is the proverb, "If man was meant to fly, we would have been given wings?" You must be willing to unlearn.

If you know where you'd like to go, you may very likely start out with only a vague view of the path to success or an abundance of possible paths. When that happens do these:

❖ Take the first few steps.
❖ Keep your eyes on the goal.
❖ Follow your chosen path as long as it gets you closer to the goal.
❖ As you approach, you'll see the path more clearly or see better route(s) among the options. If you do, change direction as needed.
❖ Keep going despite potholes, mud puddles, fallen trees, distractions, and the like.
❖ Each step is like a log on one of those old footbridges. You will eventually step on enough individual logs to

cross the bridge from where you are to where you want to be.

Planning is not *good practice*—it is *vital*. Without a plan, you'll waste time, effort, money, and other resources, and you'll try the boss' patience. However, I've often seen people wasting significant time on making plans that are too detailed and consider too many risks and possible scenarios. In each project, you need to discover the "sweet spot" that balances planning and doing. If you just keep planning, you'll never reach your end goal, or you'll get there too late.

Of course, this only works if you know where you're going. What's your vision? Can you describe what success looks like? To develop a strategy and to execute that strategy are equally important even if many things are obscure at the beginning—and maybe, on occasion, in the middle. Remember, when you execute, you create friction. Friction, like that between a tire and the road, is required for movement. It fosters progress. Here's one other point here:

Fake it till you make it.

Even if you don't know exactly every step you need to take, get your butt in gear and move! You can't be afraid of taking steps that might not be ideal. It's better to move in a zigzag manner towards your goals (in fact, that's far more likely than a straight line) versus standing still and forever contemplating the optimal path to get to the goal.

Can You Do Hardware without Software?

Start-ups often struggle to bridge the gap between their product or service and their customers. I learned this the hard way while serving as vice president of marketing at Discretix from 2004 to 2005.[5]

We developed cybersecurity hardware to be integrated into semiconductor chips designed by others. Our goal was simple: get our customers (companies that developed things like smartphones, flash drives, and USB sticks) to integrate our hardware into their systems. We—Gal Solomon, the CEO; and Edo Ganot, vice president of sales and business development; and myself—set out to sell our solution to big corporations in the USA, Europe, and the Far East.

We quickly realized that our sales cycle was long. It took months (most often, over a year) to research the customer's exact needs, demonstrate how our product filled their needs, and allow their engineers to evaluate our product. Only then was the customer comfortable enough with our hardware and software to include it in their chips and products.

Reaching this design-win involved a complex process that included educating our customers and a lot of "handholding"—helping them integrate our product into theirs. To put it simply, we never got it right on the first try. After repeating this with several customers, we identified the bridge that we had to build.

Every electronic system (computing systems, communication systems, whatever) contains hardware and software. You need both to make the system function.

---

[5] Discretix later changed its name to Sansa Security and was acquired by ARM in 2015.

Most often, the toughest part of developing and testing electronic systems lies in the interface between the hardware and the software inside the system. Think of it as two floors in a building—an upper floor of software and a lower floor of hardware. It became the industry norm to have software toolkits as the "stairs" (a bridge) between the floors. These toolkits allow the upper-floor software to most effectively use the lower-floor hardware so that the product delivers the level of functionality that the client requires.

Once we developed the software toolkits and included them in the offering to our customers, we saw a nice shortening of the sales cycle. It was suddenly much easier for our customers to integrate our solution into their products, and the time-to-value decreased dramatically. This enabled quicker design-wins and improved the scalability of our business.

We learned that developing a good product is not sufficient. You must also identify what stands between the user/customer and your product/service and bridge the gap with the missing parts. Sometimes you can do that in the development phase. At other times, you have to listen to your customers, identify the needs you missed in the initial development of your product/service, and adapt to meet them.

Chapter 2

CB&O

Coming to America

My Career—Phase 2

In March 1997, I completed my studies and graduated from Tel Aviv University with a master's of science in electrical engineering. I had, by then, seven years of professional technical experience—two with RADCOM and five in the Navy.

Since I'm an adventurous and ambitious guy, I asked myself, "What's next?" After a couple of months of discussion involving my wife, family, and friends, I concluded that the next chapter in my life would be in the business and marketing side of high tech. With this goal, I asked myself, "How do I bridge my technical expertise to business expertise—a skill set I had yet to fully develop?" Some research showed me that three things needed to happen to build this bridge between my present and my desired future:

- ❖ Move to a business/marketing role.
- ❖ Relocate to the USA because the market for high-tech products there is larger than in Israel.
- ❖ Get another degree, a master of business administration (MBA).

It took me a few years, and I achieved all three and transformed from an R&D engineer to a business & marketing executive.

My Family Bridge

Once I realized what I must do, I started looking for a business and marketing job in the USA. It was clear that it would be easier and a better fit for me to join the American office of an Israeli high-tech company. After a couple of months, I had a job offer to become an application engineer in a company called Butterfly, and my wife and I began planning our relocation to Santa Clara, California.

With the offer in hand, it was time to inform Moty Ben-Arie, then-CEO of RADCOM, of my plan to leave the company. Moty was quite surprised, as he felt I was a valuable asset to RADCOM and wondered why I wanted to leave. I explained my aspiration and need to relocate to the USA to make that happen.

"Well, if that's the case, why don't you take up a business and marketing role in our office in New Jersey and relocate over there?"

Moty soon gave me a counteroffer: to become the director of technical services at RADCOM Equipment Inc., a wholly owned subsidiary of RADCOM, responsible for North-American sales and marketing. Now I had a choice—two paths to my goal. Which would be better?

After a few more days of discussions with my wife, my parents, and some friends, Anat and I decided the RADCOM offer was the better choice. One of the reasons for this decision was, once again, based on the most important value in my life—my family. Living in New

Jersey, on the east coast, would mean only a seven-hour time difference to Israel and about ten hours of flight time. Living in California, on the west coast, would mean a ten-hour time difference and sixteen hours of flight time home, with connections making it even longer.

The shorter distance made all this much less expensive in those pre-cellular/pre-internet days. So we chose to be closer to Israel, to be closer to our family still in Israel. Indeed, the route from New Jersey to Israel became a very busy route for us and our families. During our years in America, from February 1998 through February 2002, we vacationed in Israel once or twice a year, and our relatives came to visit us at least once or twice a year.

In addition, of course, we had phone calls weekly, sometimes daily. We also exchanged video cassettes of family events so our parents would be able to see our kids as they grew up and our kids would be able to see their extended family—grandparents, uncles, aunts, and cousins.

In this case, as it was when my mom got her master's degree two decades earlier, the bridge didn't need building. But every engineer knows you don't just build and walk away. You do the needed maintenance as long as the structure lasts. It took some effort, but following my parents' example, we stayed close with our families despite the long distances between our homes.

My Experience Bridge

With my new position at RADCOM in Mahwah, New Jersey, I met and spoke to many customers and potential customers. I soon realized that many people didn't really know how to get the most value out of the products we sold them. The product was so sophisticated and versatile that it could be used for many different use cases, in many different scenarios.

I also noticed that many of RADCOM's own employees didn't really know all the features, capabilities, and the value that can be created by using our products. Both groups—external and internal—also lacked an up-to-date understanding of the ecosystem and the market.

Therefore, I started publishing *Tip of the Week*. This began as a short blurb I wrote every Friday and sent to a growing group of people. At first, it went only to the North American channel, i.e., the manufacturer reps and distributors in the USA and Canada, who sold RADCOM products. It was a group of a few dozen networking testing-solution experts, each with responsibility for a certain geography.

Tip of the Week included success stories, use cases, features, market updates, and more. The content was so compelling that many people within RADCOM asked to be added to the distribution list, and within a few months, it grew into a newsletter sent out to people in countries across the RADCOM channel globally. *Tip of the Week* became one of my "claims-to-fame," and people started approaching me to ask questions about the market and the products. I provided answers that sometimes turned into the next *Tip of the Week* as well as advice that helped close new deals and keep customers happy.

Like my earlier initiative, nobody told me to start *Tip of the Week*. I did it because I identified a need and knew an effective way to address it. As more and more people called or emailed me with questions about the market, the technologies, and RADCOM products, I quickly realized three things:

- ❖ I was frequently getting the same questions from different people.
- ❖ If two or three people asked a question, there were probably others with that question who didn't ask.
- ❖ I knew a lot more about the market, technologies, and RADCOM solutions, than others around me.

I made it a habit to review all the questions I received during each week and answer the ones that seemed most interesting and applicable to a wider audience.

Of course, this transfer of knowledge and ideas from me to others created a bridge between us. I became the go-to guy for people with questions about the market, the tech, and the products. *Tip of the Week* became a bridge that was traveled every week between the problems our staff had and the solutions our company offered, enabling them to do their jobs better and sell more products to more customers, increasing the company's revenue.

I recommend this to everybody: open your eyes and ears, identify needs within your organization or outside of it, and find effective ways to address those needs. It will be noticed.

My Educational and Network Bridges

Having relocated to America with a business and marketing role, I still had to complete the third leg of my transformation strategy—get an MBA.

During the second half of 1998, I started reviewing the different MBA programs in the USA, and it became apparent that I should focus only on executive MBA programs in what the locals called the "tristate area"— New York City and its suburbs in New York, New Jersey, and Connecticut. (Mahwah is about thirty miles from the center of New York City.) I felt that at age thirty-one, with eight years professional experience since graduating with my bachelor's, it would not make sense for me to get an MBA with young college graduates. Instead, I would go after a degree in a program with other students who were also accomplished executives.

I wasn't sure I'd be accepted to the program of my choice, so I applied to four universities—Rutgers University, Baruch College, Columbia University, and New York University. After submitting inspiring essays about what, in my mind, constituted success, I was accepted to all four. I had to decide if I was going to attend Columbia University or New York University. At that time, both were ranked in the top ten executive MBA programs in the USA.

Though Columbia ranked higher, I finally chose the NYU Stern School of Business because of the personal experience I had during the admission process. At NYU, I felt that the business school saw me as a human being and cared about me and my family. For example, my interview with Sheila Worthington, then-associate director of the executive programs, focused mainly on how my wife would cope with me keeping my day job, going to school, and being young parents of two young children. Sheila made me promise that the burden would not all go on my wife, and I did my best throughout the next two years to keep my promise.

I've never regretted for even a single minute my decision to attend NYU. The two years in the program were a life-changing event for me. I moved out of my comfort zone and learned so much from it. During those two years, I slept less than four hours a night, keeping my day job and spending one full day of study at NYU every week (alternating between Friday and Saturday). That allowed me to miss work only two days every month and miss weekends with the family only two days per month.

You might ask, "Did the sacrifice your family made return a profit?" When you enjoy what you do, it isn't a sacrifice. We considered it as an investment in our future, which brought meaning to our lives. I did need to develop a schedule that allowed me to fulfill all my obligations— my family, my employment, and my studies, in that order. I spent every possible minute with my family, studying after the kids went to sleep. On a typical day, I awoke around 5:00 a.m., read and responded to emails for an hour or two, then spent an hour with my family before driving my kids to daycare. Then I went to work, coming home between 6:00 and 7:00 p.m. to have dinner with my family. After bath time and a bedtime story, I spent three to four hours studying.

You might also ask, "Did you ever crash and burn, get overwhelmed?" I'm a naturally energetic person, which, I think, helps me keep my energy level high. We also proactively planned a work-life balance. I made (and today, still make) it a point to work on weekends only when absolutely unavoidable. The weekend is family time. I don't miss family life events, except when absolutely unavoidable. Being with my wife and kids when they achieve a milestone creates family memories and bonds, a key part of our relationship. We planned for a weeklong family vacation at least once every year, and most years, we got in two or three.

I said that in business, planning is vital. It's no less vital in the family. It may sound silly to set meetings with your children on your calendar, but it's the only way to do all the things you need and want to do. Planning reduces the urge we all have to postpone things. During some periods, when my wife and I felt we were both consumed with work and kids and everything else, we planned our couple time—we dated each other. We set aside one evening every week to go and have fun together. We put it on our calendars to ensure it was there and that we stuck to it. That kept us from setting up other things that would interfere with this precious time for ourselves.

Beyond going to Stern in Manhattan, I spent a lot of nights studying on my own and meeting with my study group and doing projects together. I experienced the power of the group and how each brought our own experience and expertise to the table. Like the Belgian draft horses, the value we created together was greater than what any of us could have done solo. The study group members were a great example of a diversified group from different cultures and disciplines:

- ❖ Lena Frank was a business development and marketing executive from Alpharma (now part of Pfizer) from the Midwest.
- ❖ Huzefa Gandhi was a product manager at Lucent who immigrated to the USA from India.
- ❖ Steve Therianos was a self-made small-business owner (Bobcats for Hire) from New Jersey.
- ❖ Jim Stanton was a director of strategic pricing at AT&T.

❖ I was the Israeli high-tech guy.

Working together on a project or assignment, each brought a different perspective, and many times, I felt I was learning more from my friends than from the professors in class. During those two years, in addition to the one-day-a-week program, we had six longer sessions that were the highlights of the program.

Four times we had a full week of study at the Doral Arrowwood Golf Resort and conference center in Rye Brook, Westchester County, New York. These were awesome weeks. Every day, we would awaken at 6:00 a.m. and go to sleep after midnight. We would study hard, really hard. Lectures, assignments, simulations, you name it! During one of these weeks, we had a full-day simulation of a medium-size business, where each student was given a role in the organization, and we were given a set of situations to deal with. I was fortunate enough to be named CEO in this simulation, and for a full day, I felt what is it like to run an American business from the top. It was quite an experience. I learned a lot about myself and the corporate culture in America.

During our last session at Arrowwood, we had a golf tournament (after all, you can't do important business in America if you don't play golf!). It was group golf, and I was lucky enough to be on the winning team. We received a trophy engraved with the winners' names and so even today, there's a golf trophy displayed somewhere at NYU with my name on it.

I'll tell you a little secret—just between us—I'm not much of a golfer, but when I learned that the next Arrowwood session would include a tournament, I wanted to be sure I didn't embarrass myself. I went on a vacation weekend with my wife to Hilton Head Island, South Carolina, and had a couple of golf lessons. I learned just enough so I know how to hold the club and swing a decent shot. Luckily, at Arrowood, my teammates were much better golfers than I was. They won the trophy, and I just tagged along.

In addition to the getaways in Arrowood, we had two longer study tours. One was ten days to the West Coast, the other was ten days in the Far East. During the West Coast trip, we visited and met with the top brass at Boeing, Microsoft, Cisco, Oracle, and others. In the Far East, we met with the top executives in Sony, NTT, and others among Japan's major players, as well as very senior executives in China of companies like the General Motors plant, local state-owned-businesses, and the Microsoft Innovation Center in Beijing. We even met the US Ambassador to China in Beijing.

During that visit to Beijing, we were fortunate enough to have a gala dinner at the Great Hall of the People—a very luxurious and majestic place. The Great Hall of the People is a state building located at the western edge of Beijing's Tiananmen Square, used for legislative and ceremonial activities by the People's Republic of China and the ruling Chinese Communist Party.

During these two study-tours, I experienced the VIP treatment of business travel of corporate America, and I had the time of my life, singing karaoke with all my American friends in Tokyo. This was an opportunity for me to connect with American leading lyrics like "Bye, bye, Miss American Pie..." and other such iconic songs.

My time at NYU was pivotal. It will affect me for the rest of my days. When we returned to Israel in 2002, I immediately looked for the Stern Alumni Club in Israel. I didn't find it because it did not yet exist. I did find one other alumnus, Saul Orbach, so we founded the Stern Alumni Club of Israel. For the first couple of years, Saul was the regional leader, then I took over. We organized many networking events, and I fostered friendships with many Stern Alumni that later became business relationships helping me (and them) professionally.

In 2014, the director of NYU Tel Aviv, Professor Benjamin "Benny" Hary, and the NYU Alumni Relations Office approached us and helped us expand the club to become the NYU Alumni Club of Israel, encompassing all NYU alumni in Israel. I volunteered and was selected as president of the club. Since then, I've had the privilege and honor to lead the leadership team of the club and join forces with exceptional alumni too numerous to name. We hosted NYU President Andrew Hamilton in Tel Aviv a couple of times with gala events that included hundreds of alumni as well as unique events with the deans of several schools including the Stern School of Business and others and smaller events with dozens of alumni, focusing on arts, law, finance, entrepreneurship, innovation, beer and wine, and other topics.

More important than all the other positives of these events, each interaction—whether social or professional—was a piece of a bridge among all these people. In effect, each of us became a girder in a vast bridge providing a pathway for alumni to create and strengthen relationships with fellow alumni. We, as humans, are naturally a little distrustful of others because some of us are naturally untrustworthy. This can be mitigated when you form a community. These bridging events gave us a personal acquaintance with potential friends and business associates that no resume can demonstrate or any due diligence can reveal.

Learning the American Ropes

Tutors and Mentors

During my time in the USA and the business side of high-tech, I learned that in sales, you lead customers through the path of least resistance, or you don't succeed. As noted already, my family spent four years in New Jersey while I worked for RADCOM Equipment Inc. During those years, I worked with several Americans who taught me the ins and outs of sales and marketing in the US. I travelled frequently around the USA and Canada, meeting with existing and potential customers. In most cases, I was accompanied by a RADCOM salesperson or one of our manufacturer's rep network members.

Jacqui McDonald, our director of marketing, for example, taught me how to write compelling text that highlighted the value and the essence of the offering, and, with her help, I published several articles in business journals and presented various seminars in conferences.

One customer visit was very special. I flew over to Chicago to meet Rich Vogt, our Midwest rep. In his private plane, Rich flew me to the John Deere headquarters in Moline, Illinois, to close the sale of some networking testing solutions. Somewhere midair, Rich gave me the steering wheel, and for the first time in my life, I flew an airplane for a short while—quite an experience.

In the tristate area (around New York City), I often traveled with Larry Scheck, our vice president of sales.

He taught me the first rule of sales, "Always Be Closing," the ABC attitude. Larry is an exceptional salesperson who can make a friend of any stranger in seconds. I remember a visit to some customers in the southern part of New Jersey. We stopped for lunch on the way. We sat down and the waitress approached us. Larry started talking with her and asked her about her kids and other personal stuff. She took our order and went off to the kitchen. The conversation between Larry and the waitress was so friendly that I had to ask Larry, "Where do you know her from?" and Larry calmly answered, "I just met her now."

Larry's ABC rule was all about how to lead your way into a corporation by identifying the path of least resistance and driving hard through that path with a sharp focus on closing the sale.

I also spent a lot of time with Mike Winslow who taught me that the customer is always first—notice it's not "the customer is always right." That's another old, false notion. He also showed me that you must be extremely professional, always striving to know more so you can use this know-how to help customers and potential customers. The best way to close a sale of high-end network testing solutions is to know more than your customers do about your products, the technology, and the market so you can help them solve real-life problems that are delaying the development of their next generation products.

Working in America with Americans as an Israeli required many adjustments as well as understanding of the American way of doing business. I learned many things from my boss, Avi Zamir, the president of RADCOM Equipment Inc., a former Israeli who lived and worked in the USA since the early '90s. Avi is a very smart business leader, and I learned from him the power of empowerment and how to mentor and guide people around you, whether they are your employees, managers, peers, or even customers, in a friendly yet effective manner. Avi also helped me understand how to become an effective bridge between Americans and Israelis.

Each of these tutors helped me walk across the bridge from where I was professionally to where I wanted to be. That's what mentors do.

While working for RADCOM in America, I returned to Israel to give a keynote speech at the Global RADCOM sales conference in Eilat. It was an exceptional trip for me since it was the first time I traveled to Israel without visiting family and friends. In fact, I was in Israel for just two days, and only in Eilat, at the southernmost point of the country, next to Egypt and Jordan and Saudi Arabia, on the north shore of the Red Sea. I flew from New Jersey to the Ben Gurion Airport near Tel Aviv and took a connection flight to Eilat. We stayed at one of the fancy hotels on the beach, and I gave the speech. The audience was RADCOM salespeople and our partners from Europe, South America, and the Far East.

I spoke on why we needed help from our sales channel in defining our products. I wanted to make the point that we wanted to hear the voices of the customers. Salespeople should be providing input to help guide product definitions and development of products and solutions so that we would fit better our market's needs. It was about working together, R&D and sales and marketing, to create higher value for our customers, ultimately creating greater value for our company and its stockholders.

To demonstrate this point, I did a small experiment in human behavior. I asked the audience for four volunteers. Curiously, I had two Israeli volunteers (one of them being RADCOM's CFO) and two volunteers from other countries. I took the two pairs, asked them to stand at one corner of the big hall, and told them that they needed to go to the far corner of the hall through the tables and chairs where the audience of over a hundred people were sitting.

Both pairs had one person blindfolded. I told the Israeli pair they were not allowed to talk with each other while the second pair was allowed to talk. I assumed the pair who could communicate would get to the far corner quicker than the silent pair. I wanted to show that when sales communicates with R&D, you get to the solution more quickly and effectively.

It was a good exercise to do with such a big audience, but a very risky one, and (you can guess, since I'm telling the story) the experiment failed. I made a mistake choosing two Israelis as the no-communication pair, and they reached the far corner faster than the other pair because the Israelis, although they did not know each other very well and were not allowed to talk, they helped each other very effectively. The two foreigners, unfamiliar with each other, didn't naturally work so well together. I guess the experiment showcased the chutzpah of the Israelis.

Takeaways

My time in America taught me a lot about business in America and about Americans, their culture, and their mindset. This firsthand experience became invaluable when I returned to Israel, because we did a lot of business with American companies. I learned the importance of networking and practiced it a lot. I created lifelong friendships with people. There's nothing like singing "Bye, bye, Miss American Pie..." at a karaoke place in Japan or playing at a casino in Atlantic City together to help foster close friendships.

The executive MBA program had many advantages, including the fact that everything I studied on Friday or Saturday could be implemented at my job on Monday.

I learned a lot about business leadership and political leadership. One class that had a particular impact on me was called "Leadership." We studied different leaders from world history, including Gandhi, Jack Welch, and John F. Kennedy, and how they used words and actions to lead and motivate others.

I enjoyed learning business by studying business cases of famous companies and leaders, learning about the challenges they faced and how they resolved them and created value for their stockholders.

NYU used an adaptation of apprenticeship education: "We learn by doing." We didn't just read and talk about things. We experienced them. We had to deliver presentations, develop business plans and strategies, and solve real life problems in class and as homework.

NYU also reinforced my belief in the power of community. Fellow alumni have a lot in common, memories and experiences from the same place, the same atmosphere, the same professors. People with similar backgrounds (such as being alumni of the same university) even though they have different upbringings and experiences can help each other.

Building and maintaining bridges among alumni fosters friendships that are, on a personal level, a great joy. (One can never have too many friends.) Building and maintaining the alumni club helped me create my personal brand. I became known in our community as the leader of the NYU alumni in Israel.

This brand image continues to help me advance in the business world, to build partnerships with customers, partners, investors, and employees. One example is NextLeap Ventures, which I started with my friends and colleagues from Intel and will be the focus of later chapters.

Among those NYU friends was Orit Raviv Swery, who leads Rosetta Investments, a multifamily office in Israel. When I co-founded NextLeap Ventures, we wanted to expand our investor base by reaching out to multifamily offices, and I immediately thought of Orit, a Stern Alumni Club of Israel member. We'd became good friends through the club, so it was obvious that when I wanted to partner with a multifamily office, my first choice would be Orit. Over the past several years, Orit has offered her clients opportunities to join NextLeap Ventures investments, and many have done so. This creates value for Orit and Rosetta and her clients, for me and NextLeap Ventures, and for the start-ups that NextLeap Ventures invests in. It's a win-win-win-win-win-win scenario.

Saul Orbach, who co-founded the Stern Alumni Club with me, continues to be a good friend. When he teaches MBA classes at the Technion about innovation and entrepreneurship, he sometimes calls on me to talk to his students about my experiences in these areas.

Eli Groner, another Stern MBA alumnus in Israel, used to be director general of the Prime Minister's office of the State of Israel and, for the last several years, has been managing director of Koch Disruptive Technologies, a corporate VC that invests in growth and late-stage companies. When I was looking for a keynote speaker to speak at one of the Pitch Night events we do at NextLeap Ventures, Eli was a great fit. Like Orit and Saul, Eli and I met in the Stern Alumni Club events.

Returning to Israel

In June 2001, I graduated from NYU with my MBA. Since we were the executive MBA class, our graduation ceremony was a big affair, a black-tie event at Windows on the World, the restaurant atop the North Tower (Building 1) of the original World Trade Center. You may recognize that name. The North Tower was one of the Twin Towers destroyed by the terrorist attack of September 11, 2001, just three months after our event.

The graduation ceremony was very important for me and my family. I bought myself a tuxedo, and my wife bought herself a very nice evening dress. My dad came over from Israel, just for the event, and we rented a tuxedo for him. This was a night that we all remember, a true feeling of accomplishment and pride. I was honored and felt very proud to receive the Stern Scholar recognition as well as my MBA degree during this ceremony.

Then came September 11. I remember driving to work in the morning and reaching the parking lot at the office at around 8:45 a.m., with *NPR News* on the radio. They started describing the events of that morning, and "unbelievable" doesn't begin to describe my reaction. I got out of my car and ran up the stairs to the office where the TV was already showing the amazing footage of the Twins Towers being hit and collapsing one after the other. We all realized this was not a standard morning, so we decided to close the office and go home to our families. I called my wife, and we went to take the children from their kindergarten and nursery school. On the way home, we stopped at the supermarket and bought bottled water and batteries, as it all seemed like World War III had just started and we need to be prepared for the worst.

As Israelis, we were trained to act effectively in such situations of uncertainty, without panicking. September 11 was a turning point in the life of many Americans and in my life as well. Several of my friends who worked at the World Trade Center were saved that day because they missed their morning train or had an out-of-office meeting that day. We all felt that the world would never be the same again. We had tickets to fly to Israel for the wedding of my brother Ron and his fiancé, Sharon. All flights, of course, were cancelled for several days. We did make it onto the first flight going to Israel, and it was very strange to see American security guards checking my two small kids. Amit was then just five years old, and Neta was three. They body-screened my kids as if they were actual terrorists—not an easy sight for any parent.

When we returned from that short vacation in Israel, and my brother's wedding, things were not so good in the USA. The economy started going down; many companies were losing money and letting people go. After a couple of months, we had a visit from Arnon Toussia Cohen, then-CEO of RADCOM, who came in from Israel. On his first day at the office, he called me up for a meeting and told me that RADCOM was no longer in need of my services—I was laid off. He explained that I was a very expensive executive for the company, and given the current landscape, they could no longer afford me. My role would be handled from headquarters in Israel. The whole US subsidiary would be downsized to fit the reduced revenue driven by the hurting economy.

This was a shock to me, of course, as well as every co-worker. Everybody told me that RADCOM was making a big mistake, and they would really miss me. Oddly enough, I did not take it very seriously, probably because of the strong self-confidence I developed during the executive MBA program at Stern. I briefly considered looking for another job in the USA, but after a few days, I decided that this tragedy created the perfect opportunity for my family to return to Israel.

During these days, we received video cassettes of our parents, siblings, and their children. Amit and Neta watched them on our giant television set—flat-screen TVs were years away—and the kids literally hugged the TV because they missed their grandparents, uncles, aunts, and cousins. This told us it was time to go home.

We didn't know what we'd do when we got there, but I started thinking seriously about an idea that had been percolating in my mind for a long time—to establish a start-up with one or two of my friends and develop a solution that would solve a big problem in the world. In December 2001, we decided to leave the USA.

Because we didn't have any obligations and full freedom to do whatever we wanted, we also decided that we'd take the long way home—a four-month holiday in New Zealand and Australia. We landed in Christchurch, New Zealand, rented a motorhome, and spent the most amazing two months traveling around the south and north islands. We then flew to Sydney, Australia, and spent another two amazing months touring the east coast from Sydney to Cairns. Four months in a campervan, just the four of us—two parents and two small children. This was a great bonding experience and really strengthened the relationships we had as a family.

It was like paradise. We awoke every morning without plans and with total freedom to decide if we stay or go, where we would go, and what we would do. We had all the time in the world, and we enjoyed every moment of it.

Chapter 3

CB℘

Creating Your Own Start-up

Remember, starting a company is like jumping
off a cliff and assembling an airplane
on the way down.
—Reid Hoffman,
LinkedIn co-founder and executive chairman[6]

MaxPO

MaxPO was my greatest failure and at the same time the biggest learning experience of my professional career. "MaxPO" stands for Maximum Performance Optimization. I invented it, and I'm both proud and so very happy that I went through the roller coaster of creating that business. I like Hoffman's statement, but I'd take it even further: "Starting a company is like jumping off a cliff, [*inventing*] the airplane, and assembling it on the way down."

---

[6] Reid Hoffman and Chris Yeh, *Blitzscaling: The Lightning-Fast Path to Building Massively Valuable Companies* (Glasgow: HarperCollins, 2018).

Assembling an airplane is technically easy. There are handbooks, and it's been done many times before. However, there is no handbook for a start-up.

Of course, there are thousands of books on best practices and what has worked in other start-up situations, plus many other resources that can give valuable guidance. Every start-up, however, is new and unique, and you have to learn and adapt as you go.

My initial thoughts of MaxPO started when I graduated from NYU with my MBA. The two years I went through Stern's executive MBA program were amazing. The sense of accomplishment and the things I learned about the world, about others, and about myself made me believe that I could do anything I chose to do. The entrepreneurship fire was always somewhere inside me; graduating NYU was the spark that lit my fire. First, I needed to find a problem to solve, a need to fulfill, something that would improve people's lives. After more than a decade in the world of computing and networking, it was obvious that my "something" would need to be in this sector.

I graduated in 2001, the time when home networks and SOHO (small office/home office) concepts began to emerge. Most were comprised of two or three computers, an internet modem, and a printer, all connected with cables. Being the tech geek that I am and having worked with computers and networks for years, it was only natural that relatives and friends reached out for my help in setting up these small networks. Back then, it was difficult for most people to do on their own. The configuration was complex, and you really had to know what you were doing to get it right. This, I realized, was an emerging need, a problem to solve!

Not everybody knows a tech geek who could help set up a home network, so it made sense to create software to do it for them. For a couple of months, I brainstormed with some friends, and we started to think about potential solutions to the problem. Well, as I mentioned in the last chapter, my time at RADCOM ended in late 2001, and my family decided to return to Israel. This put the start-up idea on-hold for about half a year.

We arrived home in Israel in June 2002, after the long family vacation, and the start-up bug reemerged. I started planning again. First on my list were co-founders. I knew I wouldn't be able to do it alone. As Paul Graham (co-founder of Y Combinator) wrote, "Starting a start-up is too hard for one person."[7] After four years of living in the USA, that meant meeting people and renewing relationships I had in the Israeli high-tech ecosystem. After many meetings, I chose Izik Zur as my co-founder.

Note: Choosing your co-founders must be one of your first decisions, and it must be done very carefully.

I chose Izik partly because we had history. We worked together for four years at RADCOM. We respected one another and enjoyed working together. But that was just the beginning:

❖ Izik's experience complemented mine.
❖ He's an expert in his arena—among the best software engineering managers I've known. He could architect a system, develop it, test it, and most importantly, lead other engineers in developing and testing.

---

[7] Paul Graham, "The 18 Mistakes That Kill Start-ups," Paulgraham.com (Paul Graham, October 2006), http://paulgraham.com/start-upmistakes.html.

❖ He's a very friendly person—someone you want to work with.

❖ We shared core values. We both wanted to do good in our world, solve big problems, create and capture value, make an impact, and do it all with the highest integrity.

We signed a co-founder's agreement, a very important step that should be done as early as possible even if you are very good friends, which we were, and still are.

Izik became the vice president of research and development, and I became the chief executive officer.

Over several months, we developed a business plan and the architecture of our solution, and we realized that starting the implementation would require more resources. We applied to the Ideation Tnufa Incentive Program of the Israel Innovation Authority, receiving the maximum grant. We also raised some money from two angel investors. This enabled us to hire programmers and develop a prototype.

During all this, we realized that our customers wouldn't be the consumers or small business owners; they would be internet service providers (ISPs). We developed a software solution that enabled ISPs to offer home networking services efficiently and effectively. This included provisioning, setup, configuration, and maintenance—a "plug and play" solution, we now say.

We knew from our past experience that you don't develop a solution to a problem without a close interaction with potential customers. We needed a design partner, a potential customer willing to work closely with us and help us figure out which capabilities and features would translate to the best benefit and value for our customers and end-users. Following discussions with a few Israeli ISPs, we selected Netvision, the first Israeli ISP that offered internet connectivity to homes. They were the leader in home networks, and we felt that we'd get real value from engaging with them.

They were open to this relationship and provided good feedback that helped us fine tune our solution to address the problems they were having as they rolled out home networking services. For example, in the early days of MaxPO, the solution was fully autonomous and local, embedded in the home network. By working with Netvision, it became clear that we needed to add a remote component, enabling the ISP to control things remotely.

While making great progress on creating a valuable product, we knew that we had to up our game on the business development aspects of our start-up.

I chose Ken Shostack as our business development advisor. Ken had a nice career in the USA in business development roles and helped us fine-tune our business plan as well as connect to potential investors. Ken also helped me prepare for the first business trip of MaxPO to Philadelphia. This was really exciting. I travelled on my own, with a demo system on my laptop, to meet with Comcast, then the largest home ISP in the USA. They really liked our solution, and we started a relationship with them. During this business trip, I also met with several potential investors—angels and VCs—in Boston and New York.

The feeling I had during this trip was something I remember to this day. It felt so good to be showing my baby—MaxPO—to the world. I was proud of myself, our team, and the solution we've developed. It felt good. On the other hand, it was a bit scary and lonely at times. Nobody told me what to do or where to go. I had the full freedom and responsibility to do what I thought was right. I felt that my years in high tech in Israel and the US had prepared me well for this. I was self-confident.

This, however, wasn't my first investor undertaking. We met with many VCs in Israel, and our most advanced discussions were with Cedar Ventures. Nimrod Schwartz wasn't just a partner at Cedar Ventures; he'd been a co-founder, vice president of business development, and chief technology officer of Netvision. He understood exactly what MaxPO set out to do. He had personally experienced the challenges of an ISP in rolling a new service into the homes of consumers. But it seemed he wasn't sure we were the best team to solve these challenges. We presented Nimrod a business plan that required $1 million to get to initial revenue from Comcast in the USA. He counteroffered with $500,000 for a more limited, scaled-down milestone. I thought he was testing us to see if we are confident of our plan and ability to execute, so I turned down his offer. He built a bridge right in front of me, and instead of walking across to shake his outstretched hand, I burnt it down.

This was probably the biggest mistake I made, but it became one of the most important lessons I learned: don't say no to an investor who wants to give you money!

It was too little and couldn't get us to where we really wanted and needed to be. However—and this is the moral of the story—it would've gotten us *somewhere*, and *somewhere* is closer than *nowhere*.

❖ Getting that half-million dollars would have enabled us to make progress on many fronts.

❖ It would have strengthened our relationship with Cedar Ventures so they would invest more in the future.

❖ People tend to want to go second, to follow rather than lead, even among angels and VCs. Had we accepted Cedar Ventures' offer, other more hesitant investors would have felt more at ease about joining the financing, enabling further progress.

Refusing the money from Cedar Ventures was a colossal mistake, and I made it because I thought like a mathematician and not like an engineer. Remember the cake story from Chapter 1? Same story, different players. If you think you'll never get there, you don't start. If you know you'll get *close enough*, you run forward. More than any other lesson, I realized it's massively important to keep moving forward even if you have to take smaller steps along the way—you need to constantly make progress toward your end-goal.

One of the potential investors I met with was Daniel Star of Intel Capital, who also connected me with other Intel executives. In March 2003, Intel launched its Centrino platform, paving the way for wireless local area networks (LANs). Wi-Fi LANs, as they're now called, got rid of the cables, making home networks that much easier for consumers to set up, and that made it much more popular. It also made home networks more complex to configure and troubleshoot. So Intel started searching for start-ups that had solutions to this problem. Daniel and I had a good connection from the beginning of the discussion. I felt they understood what MaxPO was doing and how our solution could help proliferate home networks across the globe, exponentially increasing the demand for laptops using the Intel Centrino platform.

After several months of engagement with Intel Capital (it was now late 2003), we realized Intel was also looking at another company that just started claiming they could do what we claimed we could do. Gteko, our competitor, began in 1992 and had, at that point, a hundred employees that were mainly focused on other software business, not related to home networks IT. We started working on our solution almost two years before they did, but they had more experience, better connections, and a bigger team, so they made quicker progress. Ultimately, Intel (and others) invested in Gteko to the tune of about $10 million.

MaxPO ran out of money early in 2004, so Izik and I made the heartbreaking decision to shut it down. We just hadn't raised the money we needed. It was a sad moment, and we felt the heartache of failure. Nevertheless, it was a great learning experience, and I don't regret having spent these two years focusing on MaxPO.

The After-Max

Following MaxPO, I became a consultant and advisor to several start-ups, helping them formulate their strategy, establish their business, and drive their product definition and marketing.

My friend and partner, Izik Zur, joined Gteko, helping them complete the development of their home networking IT support system, bringing our MaxPO to their system. In September 2006, Microsoft acquired Gteko for around $100 million, as part of its strategy to establish an R&D center in Israel. Since that time, the Microsoft

Operating System included concepts, features, and capabilities that were part of the home network IT solution that we envisioned at MaxPO.

By this time, I was working at Intel, and it was a bittersweet moment for me. On the one hand, it confirmed that MaxPO addressed an important problem and need and provided a real solution for it. On the other hand, it confirmed the importance of execution, experience, and pragmatic thinking that we lacked at MaxPO.

While creating MaxPO, I built a lot of bridges. However—again, this is vital—I didn't build enough bridges, nor did I build bridges that reached our desired destination. I take full responsibility for that failure, but even though the experience didn't get where we hoped it would arrive, I'm happy it was a chapter in my life.

After MaxPO, I spent some time with Discretix as VP of marketing and did some consulting gigs while I contemplated the next phases in my career. I felt that among the things I wanted to learn was how to behave and achieve results in the corporate environment, an environment which always comes with a political landscape. The obvious solution would involve working for a major international corporation. I reached out to many of my connections, including Daniel Star (from Intel Capital), and he connected me with the strategic planning organization at Intel, which ultimately led me to join Intel as a senior strategic planner in January 2006.

Chapter 4

CB ED

The Multinational Corporation Way

Why Join a Multinational Corporation?

In 2006, after eleven years in start-ups, I joined the chip giant Intel. Founded in 1968, it's been the world's largest semiconductor company for many years, and one of the founding companies of Silicon Valley and the high-tech sector. My decision hinged on two goals:

❖ If you want to have a big impact on the world and leave a legacy, you can invent something new, establish a start-up, and focus on it for many years until it becomes successful. Alternatively, you can join a multinational corporation (MNC) that already has a big footprint and impact in the world. As part of an MNC, you can lead innovation from within, leveraging the scale and reach that a major player already has.

❖ I'd been in start-ups for most of my career, and I came to feel that I lacked a needed skill set. I needed to learn how to behave and achieve results in a corporate environment, where all kinds of political things happened. I take a very pragmatic view of office politics. I don't call it a good thing or a bad thing. I feel that the minute you have two or three people involved in something, there's at least some politicking. For better and for worse, it's there, and it's not going away. Therefore, you have to deal with it. Stressing over it and debating the morality is pointless. You simply have to make the politics work to be successful.

According to the late Clayton Christensen, there are two types of innovation—linear, incremental innovation and disruptive, exponential innovation.[8] MNCs typically focus on linear innovation by developing the next generation of existing product lines. In these types of product lines, the value grows linearly over time, as you move from one generation to the next one. Start-ups, on the other hand, typically focus on disruptive innovation. They develop product lines providing value that grows exponentially over time, as you move from one generation to the next one. That said, research shows that the MNCs that allocate all their budget to incremental innovation will eventually decline, replaced by companies providing better solutions. MNCs that spend 10 to 25 percent of their R&D budget on disruptive innovation are more successful financially, maintaining their leadership position for longer.

I had the privilege of working at Intel on both types. I led the product definition of several next-generation product lines, and I led the identification and incubation

---

[8] Clayton M. Christensen, *Innovator's Dilemma: When New Technologies Cause Great Firms to Fail* (Boston, M.A.: Harvard Business School Press, 1997).

of strategic new technologies that are transforming markets or sometimes creating whole new markets.

Shortly after I joined Intel, they assigned me as the first strategic planner of their new Atom™ product line. Atom™ is a family of low-power, low-cost CPUs for a number of target segments, including, among other things, netbooks (low-power, low-cost laptops), embedded systems, and smartphones.

At that time, Intel was very naïve and inwardly-focused—one might even say arrogant—as the company was king of the hill in all things CPU-related. This was not a good thing, and being top of the industry was no excuse. Most people at Intel believed that they actually knew better than any of the customers or original equipment manufacturers (OEMs), so discussions with potential customers were few and didn't have much influence on Intel's products.

Intel had become a corporation with its own language, customs, and way of doing things—many times, a very different way than the rest of the industry. For example, I was hired to lead the vision, segmentation, target market definition, product definition, requirements, and specifications to guide R&D and help sales and marketing penetrate the market. Intel called this position "strategic planner," while most other high-tech companies would have called me "product manager." I called me "Builder of Bridges" across the different groups within the organization and between the organization and external entities, such as customers and partners.

After working in that capacity since the early 1990s, starting when I served in the navy, I knew that a lot of my interaction would be with external entities—end-users, customers, and partners. So, on my first day at Intel, I asked for business cards. I was surprised to be told, "You don't need business cards at Intel; all you need is your Intel blue badge." In those days, strategic planners at Intel didn't have much interaction with the outside world.

I was also surprised to hear feedback from my co-workers when I told them I'm doing "mobile strategic planning." They said something like, "No, you don't understand. 'Mobile' is 'laptops and notebooks'; you're doing 'handheld' strategic planning." Intel was so disconnected from the industry it was trying to penetrate that they didn't even know how the rest of the industry was talking about itself.

Nevertheless, I was very impressed during the hiring process. I never met with a professional human resources person. I met with the hiring manager, Arie Harsat, along with his supervisor, Yoav Hochberg, and his director, Alex Peleg. All three were very impressive, and I felt I could learn from all of them. These interviews made me feel I was coming into the right place for me, that I would learn a lot about corporate America, and we'd do great things together. That is, in fact, what happened, and I spent a very exciting and fruitful eleven years with Intel.

Strategic Planning

Defining Winning Products

Strategic planning is all about defining winning products. This requires building many bridges. It starts with the art of innovation—the bridge I discussed before between problems, needs, and solutions. It needs to solve a problem and *create value*, but that's not enough. For innovation to succeed in the marketplace, it needs to *capture value.* That means monetizing the solution by solving the problem/need in a way that the marketplace can afford and will respond to by paying for the solution.

Solving problems, by itself, is a nice academic project that never goes beyond the theoretical or experimental phase. For innovation to scale globally, there needs to be a business that can profitably sell the solution to the target market and perhaps expand that market.

One of the things that impressed me about Intel was the long lines of gray cubicles and the huge number of them. Nobody at Intel had an office. Even the high-level executives had an open cubicle. I later learned these gray cubicles looked almost the same in every Intel site—Santa Clara, California; Hillsboro, Oregon; Haifa, Israel; and all the others. The scale of the whole company impressed me, as I'd always worked in small or medium-sized start-ups—groups of dozens or hundreds of employees.

At Intel, it was tens of thousands. I wasn't sure about how to behave in such a large organization. Fortunately, like any other new employee at Intel, I had a "buddy." The buddy system is important. It's Intel's way of integrating new employees. My buddy was a peer with years of experience working at Intel, and he knew the ins and outs of the organization. Whenever I had a question or topic to discuss that I didn't feel I could discuss with my manager, I went to my buddy. Mainly, it was logistics and bureaucratic things, but not exclusively. For example, I asked my buddy, "In such a large organization, there must be some kind of bylaws or guidebook on what is right and what is wrong—where can I find this?" His answer was simple but profound. He said:

- ❖ At Intel, you can do whatever you want and say whatever you want as long as it meets two criteria:
  - o You're ready to tell your child about it tonight.
  - o You're ready to have it published in the newspaper tomorrow morning.
- ❖ If it meets those two criteria, it's okay—you can say it; you can do it.

This is a great example of the Intel values. Integrity is very important; it is the foundation of relationships between people. Integrity is the cement that holds the bridges between people together over the long-term.

In this position, my partner, manager, and mentor was Arie Harsat. Arie taught me how to think in a big corporation like Intel and how to navigate your way to get things done on a large scale. He taught me the importance of data-driven analysis and decision-making. At Intel, it was always important to use data when driving toward a decision. Never wave your hands; this isn't sustainable. It might convince some people, some of the time, but if you want to convince all the people, all the time, you must stick to facts, data, and logic. For example, Arie taught me a strategic decision-making method with steps that are simple to define yet difficult to perform:

- ❖ Articulate a clear and succinct definition of the strategic question at hand:
  - o What is the decision that needs to be made?
  - o Why should it be done now?
- ❖ Define the key metrics for measuring the success of the outcome of the decision.
- ❖ Identify the options and possible outcomes of different options.

❖ Grade each of the options vs. the key metrics for that outcome. (Colors sometimes help: green means meets or exceeds the requirement; yellow means barely meets requirements; red means doesn't meet requirement.)

Typically, the right decision will jump out almost naturally from a table like this:

Metrics	Requirement	Option 1	Option 2
Performance	>100	120	102
Power	<10	10	15
Cost	$8–10	$8	$10
Size	200 x 200	205 x 195	220 x 180
Time to Implement	18 months	18 months	24 months

Dark Gray = Doesn't Meet; Moderate Gray = Barely Meets; Light Gray = Meets or Exceeds

Of course, tables in the real world are much more complex. Yet it's the work of the strategic planner to simplify them without losing content to the point where the decision making can be fast and easy.

At Intel, I learned how to use several fundamental elements that enable the definition of winning products. The most important among those are the product overview proposal (POP) and the landing zone (LZ). (These were in-house Intel terms; other companies may use different terms.) These tools and methodologies serve as a bridge between ideas, value, and people.

One final note: Looking back to our discussion of meetings and minutes, I repeat that communication is key. It is the bridge that ultimately crosses all human gaps, but most particularly, with complex projects that involve many people. Verbal communication is how most communication occurs, but words evaporate on the wind. Every important communication must be preserved. As many have suggested, "If it isn't written down, it didn't happen."

I'd like to emphasize that written communication is not important simply because it leaves a "paper trail" (important for legal and other reasons), but also because it drives effective collaboration and execution of complex projects.

Landing Zone

Before we get into the strategic planning process, I want to describe the landing zone. The LZ model is the tool we used to specify and track product requirements as part of strategic planning, development, testing, and production. An LZ is comprised of the full set of requirements: key product indicators (KPIs), features, technologies, capabilities. The LZ outlines three distinct specifications for each requirement:

❖ **Minimum**. This is the hard deck. If a product falls below these specifications, it starts to be questioned. In some cases, when it makes sense, one or very few items are defined as a "kill switch"—if we don't meet a certain requirement, the product is cancelled.

❖ **Target**. These are the specifications that enable the product to *deliver the forecasted financial results* (mainly volume, revenue, and profit) and meet the anticipated R&D budget, product cost, and schedule.

❖ **Outstanding**. These are the requirements that provide *substantial additional value*—the level at which a product has the potential to generate *considerably* higher financial value over the target.

The LZ

❖ includes proper justification for every item;
❖ describes what the previous generation provides and what the competition provides; and
❖ specifies all product aspects, such as schedule, cost, segments, performance, power, size, features, and more.

The LZ incorporates inputs and considerations from many domains:

❖ Market trends, competition, and usage models
❖ Improvement over the previous generation (called "Goodness" at Intel), and the focus of the product
❖ Technologies and manufacturing capabilities that are available

For Intel LZs, requests from the different internal customers—the Personal Computing Client Group (PCCG), the Data Center Computing Group (DCG), the Embedded Computing Group (ECG), and the Software and Systems Group (SSG)—represented external customers. Each had provided inputs into all LZ definitions, enabling a converged solution that can optimally address all of them.

Product Overview Proposal

The POP is the all-inclusive process of defining products at Intel. It's the bridge connecting all the people working on a product line, aligning them on a coherent path converging to a well-defined product that provides a compelling solution to customer needs and wants and creates profit.

Though my work on POPs was entirely in a high-tech environment, I include a detailed explanation here because creating a POP builds a bridge among all stakeholders that will enable creating and capturing value. This process can be adapted to meet the needs of almost any project planning group and almost any project.

I led POP creation for several product lines at Intel and wrote the first draft of the *POP Cookbook*—a detailed guideline that describes and explains all the intricacies of the POP, what it is and how it is done. This became the bridge Intel used in many future projects. It was used and updated by many strategic planners at Intel to ensure the knowledge passed among all strategic planners, both veterans and new hires just starting. I am proud to say that this particular bridge that I built has been traversed by many people as they led the definition of Intel's product lines.

The POP is created by an interdisciplinary team focused on developing feasible product definitions to maximize value for the company. These product definitions need to adhere to several criteria:

❖ They need to align with the company's vision, strategy, business, and competitive environment.
❖ They need to make business sense. They should lead to growth of market segment share (MSS), average selling price (ASP), and margin (profit*).
❖ The POP specifies, in detail, product feature set as well as the feasible execution plans, milestones, and schedule.

*Profit is typically defined in financial terms; however, there are other occasions where profit can be defined differently. For example, value can be provided to society through nonprofit organizations, or value might be provided to humanity and our planet in sustainability projects. In my opinion, there's no such thing as a "nonprofit" group or project. We simply define profit differently in different situations.

The POP is a very delicate balancing act, mixing innovation and risk management so that we plot the best course to that profit. The POP includes several phases (levels) that are brought to relevant executive management for approval at appropriate milestones:

POP L0: Market Environment, Trends, and Road Map Intercept

Level 0 includes high-level goals and segmentation through a market environment assessment based on trends, emerging usage models, and competitive threats. This phase identifies long-lead technology improvements for path finding—exploration of the research and development teams. Finally, L0 bridges from the wishful thinking of the dream product to the reality of practical constraints.

The POP also defines and approves the scope of changes of the product line, i.e., how big is the development budget for the product.

POP L1: Product Requirements and Initial Direction

L1 includes the definition and agreement among all stakeholders involved on the LZs, using minimum-target-outstanding measures for all aspects of the product (usages, hardware, software, firmware, user experience, form factor, and more). It also includes a list of techno-logical improvements that require development and in-tegration. Finally, it includes the architecture strawman proposal and its approval as a framework under which the product will be developed. The LZ is established and ratified in POP L1 by a relevant decision-making forum. After POP L1, any LZ change will require that same deci-sion-maker approval.

POP L2.X: Key Implementation Decisions

There might be multiple L2 milestones (L2.1, L2.2, and so on) in which the POP team brings to management the key plan of record (POR) changes for approval in order to streamline and refine the definition of the product as the development progresses. Many times, this includes key trade-off decisions impacting where the product will land in the LZ. In one of these milestones, a preliminary "die strategy" will be developed and approved. A die, in the context of semiconductors, is a block of semiconducting material on which certain integrated circuits are fabricated. When you develop a semiconductor product line, you typically have several dies developed, each with somewhat different feature sets and key performance indicators to enable segmentation and optimization of value, features, cost, and time to market.

POP L2 is where engineering comes back with the LZ response, and we set POR, specifically: Where do we land on the LZ that was approved in L1? The product should meet targets for every item, ideally; however, there will be areas where circumstances require that we just meet the minimum. If there are too many items where we only meet minimum, the product must be re-evaluated. The POP team may decide to redirect the product—that is, change the schedule, the R&D investment, remove features, or cancel the product altogether. If that seems to be the way to go, this recommendation will be brought to executive management, which may decide to pull the kill switch.

POP L2 Final: The 90 Percent Feature Freeze

This milestone comprises the full engineering response and POR of the product line. The LZ is graded for usages, hardware, software, and all other aspects. This is the final and detailed definition of the product; accepting the L2 Final triggers spending—significantly more spending (head count, equipment, etc.)—to do the actual development of the product. Before POP L2 Final, you might have many dozens of people working on a product line, maybe a few hundreds. After POP L2 Final, you start growing the teams to many hundreds and then thousands of people. It also includes the final prioritized technologies that should be developed as part of the product to ensure the required value is delivered to different customers.

POP L2 Final is a very big and important milestone. After it completes, making changes that are too dramatic will cause significant impact to spending, schedule, and ultimately, the value that the product line brings to the market and the financial returns for the company.

POP L3: Executable POR and SKU (Stock Keeping Unit) Plan

This is the final phase of product definition. It ensures that all features, schedules, development and testing plans, funding, and resources are in place. In this important milestone, you also define a detailed SKU plan. This details the different variants of the product, what markets or customers they'll target, what features and key performance indicators they'll have, what volume will be required to manufacture, and what the product pricing strategy will look like.

A POP L3 includes the ecosystem-enabling plan—software enabling the product and any other type of activities that need to be performed to ensure it will be easy to sell the product in big volumes. Typically, when you complete POP L3, the strategic planner hands off the ownership of the product to the program manager responsible for execution of the plan.

Post-POP L3: Execution

The strategic planning team continues to support the execution of the product line, driving key strategic decisions as needed.

Each of the POP milestones typically takes several month; however, I've lead POPs that took over three years to complete and one POP that was done fully in one day. It was one very long day, from 7:00 a.m. to 11:00 p.m. The POP team included a couple dozen very senior and experienced people, representing all relevant disciplines. It had the approval of four Intel VPs, each responsible for a specific part of the puzzle. It was for a product code-named Faith that was to be a system-on-chip (SoC) for smartphones, with full integration of the communications capabilities, computing, and other system capabilities. Despite that spectacular effort by a great team, the product wasn't funded at the right time, and it's part of the reason Intel lost the smartphone market to its competitors.

The Organization of the POP team

The organization of the POP team is critical to success. The POP should be led by a strategic planner who should be senior, experienced, and smart—in technology, in business, and, most of all, in people. The strategic planner leading the POP team is the bridge. He or she spearheads the definition of the product line. He or she needs to be highly networked and knowledgeable about the company, the competition, the technologies, the customers, and the industry as a whole.

Roles and responsibilities of the POP lead include the following:

- ❖ To lead product (or product line) definition to maximize value for the organization
- ❖ To provide clear, detailed recommendations to executive management of product definition and feasible execution plans
- ❖ To lead, motivate, and align the multidisciplinary product definition teams toward a common vision and ensure clear understanding of the vision and strategy
- ❖ To ensure that highest-value capabilities are integrated into products at the right intercept point for

a sustained competitive advantage leading to MSS, ASP, and margin growth

❖ To drive the different teams to a balanced mix of innovation and risk management and identify and resolve tensions to ensure an effective and efficient process

The POP team should include senior experts and managers from all disciplines involved in the product definition, development, testing, manufacturing, marketing, and support. At Intel, the POP team usually included technologists, systems engineers, architects, designers, validation, verification, manufacturing, quality, and reliability, marketing, sales, support, and finance. It should include experts on all the ingredients of the product, including hardware, firmware, software, algorithms, and every other aspect. It should also include the business people (both sales and marketing), those who are close to the customers and end-users and know how to market and sell the product once it is ready.

The POP lead typically sets a recurring meeting— weekly, biweekly, monthly, or other—in order to keep the POP team in sync. A typical Intel POP also included several different work groups (WGs) that contributed to the POP. Such work groups will focus on different aspects of the product. For example, when I led the definition of Skylake (Intel's sixth generation CORE™ product line), the POP included quite a few WGs—competitive WG, media WG, graphics WG, technologies WG, software WG, security and manageability WG.

The POP lead, you might say, becomes the conductor of a large orchestra, with brass, percussion, strings, and woodwinds, except that this ensemble is writing the music, not just playing it. Imagine composing Beethoven's Fifth Symphony or Tchaikovsky's 1812 Overture by committee! It may sound like a ridiculous thing, but it can be very effective if it is done in the right way.

At Intel, a technology readiness process (TRP) acted in parallel to the POP. The TRP ensured the maturity and value of new technologies were optimized. The TRP is typically managed by a forum called Intel Product Technology Readiness (IPTR).

Not everything went through a TRP. Any technology, new or modified, that posed a risk to the products being developed should go through the readiness process. Typically, these are technologies that affect CPU/platform architecture require changes to one or more platform layers, interact with other planned or existing technologies, require external hardware/software enabling, have cross-segment or multigenerational impact, seek to enable new value propositions and business models, and other such challenges.

In some cases, "readiness" might have to deal with changing government regulations, influencing industry standards or creating partnerships with other ecosystem travelers. The key is to consider any internal and external forces that may impact the product or service.

Technologies that didn't require TRP were those that were either evolutionary (making an incremental change over a previous generation) or highly self-contained (that is, micro-architecture of the internals of the CPU). Such technologies were declared "TRP N/A" with the agreement of IPTR. Whenever there was doubt, a formal waiver from IPTR was the way to go. It was important not to bypass the TRP process—it's like getting a second opinion in major medical decisions or doing due diligence in a legal matter. Leaving out this check rarely comes to a good end. What's worse, shortcuts create unknown risks and can lead to considerable waste of resources.

Earlier, I noted that in Israel, we tend to seek forgiveness rather than permission. When dealing with new technologies, there is often no forgiveness to be had. CPU product development and testing is very complex, and even in the high-tech sector, most people don't fully understand all the interdependencies and risks associated.

Chapter 5

᎕ᏁᏅ

An "Atomic" Education

This chapter (as well as some following chapters) includes a great deal of technical information necessary to the story, but I remind you, the technology is not the story. The story is what I learned from some successful and unsuccessful projects during my time at Intel.

ATOM™ is Intel's low-power CPU product line targeting small, affordable systems. From 2006 to 2008, I had the privilege to be the first strategic planner of the ATOM™ brand for three full years. I led the definition of several product lines that targeted new market segments, along with a spectacular team of individuals. I worked closely, collaborated with, and learned a lot from Dan Cohen, the lead platform strategic planning manager (my friend and later a partner at NextLeap Ventures); VP Elinora Yoeli, the general manager of the Intel Austin engineering team; Intel Fellow Belli Kuttanna and Rajesh Patel, the lead CPU and SoC architects; Intel Fellow Ticky Thakkar, the lead platform architecture manager; and VP Haytham Samarachi, the design team manager.

Defining a New Product Line

My first lesson in corporate politics didn't take long after I joined Intel in January 2006. My initial project at Intel (in early 2006) was called Dehlin, a CPU core designed to be integrated into several different system-on-chip developed by Intel and targeting different segments:

❖ Silverthorne CPU, which targeted the ultra-mobile PC (UMPC) and netbook markets
❖ Shawnigan, which targeted the high-end phone or handheld device (now called smartphones) market.
❖ Other SoC markets for embedded and broadband-access devices

Shawnigan was based on an existing SoC that Intel's Cellular Handheld Group (CHG) was already selling to customers, like the Palm Pilot. CHG had been acquired by Intel in 1999. When Intel sold CHG, just a few months after I started there, it was the end of the Shawnigan program, which effectively killed the Dehlin project overall, as none of the other Intel business units were willing to fund creation of such low-power, low-cost products, even though they could've been integrated into many different types of SoCs.

I learned that when you work in a big corporation like Intel, you can do an excellent job, but there are things that you can't control. They are beyond your circle of influence, or as they say, "above my pay grade." Cancellation of a project should not discourage you or make you feel depressed. It is quite common in the high-tech world. You must learn what you can from each project and move on to the next.

This is why the mindset of people working in big corporations is quite different from people working for small start-ups. In an MNC, relationships with co-workers are more important than meeting goals and objectives of any given project. Projects come and go, and some get cancelled before they're completed. When they do, the team goes their separate ways. However, you'll probably work with those same people on some succeeding project, so you'd better have a great relationship with former teammates. If not, working effectively with them over the long haul gets very difficult.

The second product line under my responsibility was Silverthorne. This was the first low-power CPU chip that Intel developed targeting netbooks, UMPCs, mobile internet devices (MIDs), and low-end desktops. It was part of the Menlow platform. I became involved toward the end of the program and led the definition of the segmentation and SKU strategy in the POP L3 phase of Silverthorne.

We solved several issues in the definition of the product line and developed a seven-SKU strategy that improved the market value of the products. In start-ups, I was used to revenues in the tens of millions, but Silverthorne brought in more than $1 billion in revenue during the first year after launch. I remember the feeling—it was exhilarating! Later, I realized that the ATOM™ product line was only a small portion of the overall Intel revenue stream, most of which came from the CORE™ product lines.

After Silverthorne, I led the definition of Lincroft, an SoC for MIDs. Earlier, I mentioned two types of innovation—linear and disruptive—and that major players focused on linear while start-ups generally work toward disruptive. In working on Silverthorne, I learned that Intel always compared the value of the potential product versus the previous generation instead of versus competitors. The definition of Lincroft required changing these two Intel paradigms, as this was a product line that was disruptive and did not have a prior generation at Intel to compare with.

Lincroft was the first CPU-Hub—that is, we realized we could provide better value, higher performance, lower power, and lower cost by integrating the graphics, video, display, and memory into the CPU and develop an SoC that included all the processing elements and most of the interfaces to the other chips in the system. This was a big (dare I say, disruptive?) shift in the architecture of Intel CPUs that later moved from the ATOM™ product line to the CORE™ product lines and impacted the overall architecture of computing systems.

As part of the Lincroft definition, I brought into the strategic planning toolset the "spider diagram" (also called a "radar chart") showing the value of the product compared to competitors' products on a number of dimensions. We included the most important attributes for a smartphone: connected standby time (impacts the "battery life"—that is, the time of use before charging is required), thermal design point (impacts the form-factor—that is, the physical dimensions), cost, area, compatibility with existing Intel software, CPU performance, graphics performance, video performance, display resolution, and the level of integrated communications. In this case, we didn't compare our product to Intel's previous products. We compared it to Texas Instruments' OMAP and Qualcomm's Snapdragon SoCs. This was a first for

Intel, and the bridge-building processes I described earlier were a major component of those successes.

My last project in the ATOM™ world was leading the definition of Penwell, another SoC—Intel's first attempt at developing an IA-based SoC, specifically designed for smartphones. IA stands for Intel Architecture, the CPU hardware architecture Intel developed to enable the x86 CISC (complex instruction set computer). We integrated all the functionalities of the system into a single chip, including CPU, graphics, video, audio, imaging, display, memory, security, and I/O. We did this during 2008 (the POP took one year, which was a record time for a definition of an Intel product line), intending for it to hit the market in 2010. If it had, it would've been the best SoC for smartphones at that time. However, due to execution issues, it wasn't launched to market until 2012, by which time, it was no longer competitive.

Penwell taught me, and all of Intel, a great lesson—timing! When you define and develop a product, it must hit the market on the target launch date to ensure it addresses the market for which it was designed. Innovation in high-tech is progressing rapidly, more rapidly with every passing year. Significant delays mean you must re-evaluate your product in light of recent market changes and decide if it makes sense to continue, alter course, or go to the ultimate extreme—cancel the product even though you've already spent millions of dollars developing it. Sometimes it is better to cut your losses and move to a different path toward fulfilling your vision and increasing your profits.

Intel failed to pay attention to the rapidly changing mobile market, and lost that market.

Why Didn't Apple Use Intel Chips in iPhones/iPads?

Intel had a great partnership with Apple, but only partially. In 2005, Apple announced it would switch to Intel chips for its Macs beginning in 2006 and would transition all Macs to Intel chips by 2007. (Apple had been using PowerPC chips in Macs.) However, when Steve Jobs introduced the first iPhone on January 9, 2007, it wasn't using an Intel CPU, it used an ARM CPU in a SoC manufactured by Samsung.

In early 2008, Apple and Intel discussed using Intel's solution for the iPhone. Intel, however, wasn't very receptive because company leaders at that time didn't understand the unique requirements of an SoC for smartphones compared to chips for notebooks and laptops. Intel pitched the Silverthorne ATOM™ chip as the CPU for the iPhone, and I recall many discussions where I tried to explain to others at Intel why this wasn't a good fit:

Silverthorne was not a fully integrated SoC. It required other chips on the motherboard. This meant more components, which meant more space on the board (not a good thing in a handheld device) and more power consumed, resulting in a shorter battery life—less than a full day under normal conditions.

This engagement is what drove Intel to start developing a new, fully integrated SoC, Penwell, which would meet the requirements of the smartphone. I was the lead strategic planner of Penwell, but as I mentioned, that was a little too late.

As the Penwell project was moving forward during the early months of 2008, we worked closely with Apple as it explored the use of Intel's x86 SoC for their next generation of iPhone and their first-generation iPad. We "opened the kimono" and told them everything we knew about semiconductor design, testing, and manufacturing. After a weeklong face-to-face meeting with them at our Austin site in April 2008, Apple announced it had acquired a company called P. A. Semi, which would be designing Apple's own SoC instead of buying from Intel.

This was very disappointing for all of us. We later learned that there were other high-level discussions between Apple CEO, Steve Jobs, and Intel CEO, Paul Otellini. In those discussions, Apple wanted two things that Intel was not willing to provide:

❖ Significantly lower prices than what Intel thought it should get. Intel was thinking the smartphones and tablets markets were the same as the PC market, which is far from true.

❖ Apple wanted to provide Intel with silicon IP blocks that Intel would integrate into our SoC. Apple didn't want to reveal what these IP blocks did or how they operated. Intel was accustomed to being a fully-vertically integrated manufacturer, controlling all the design, testing, and manufacturing. Intel was not willing to let Apple provide parts for the SoC that were like black boxes because Intel would never be able to verify that those black boxes functioned as designed.

As a result, the talks broke down, and Apple took a different path. Intel never again came close to dominating the mobile market as it had dominated other markets.

Why Did Intel Miss the Smartphone Revolution?

The proliferation of mobile communication and computing—smartphones—was one of the biggest tech revolutions in history. It has impacted humanity on a global and historical scale. Intel was already the king of personal computing and data center computing, and many people, including Intel executives, expected Intel to become the world's smartphone leader as well. Intel tried to offer a compelling solution for smartphones but failed miserably.

I've been privy to some of the work done at Intel in this area and developed my own understanding of the big question: Why did Intel fail? Others involved and those viewing from outside may have reached different conclusions, but from my perspective, there were several fundamental misconceptions that caused Intel to miss the mobile revolution:

First, an Arrogant Attitude

"We know it all." Many at Intel thought that we were better and smarter than our customers and that we didn't really have any competitors. Imagine a distant cousin, whom you love but only see once a year or so, comes in and starts giving you advice, saying he knows your immediate family better than you do. You'd be annoyed, at the very least. Well, that's how our customers, OEMs like Apple, Samsung, and others, probably felt. They know their market and their products, and they didn't appreciate another company thinking it knew better than they did.

Second, Unrealistic Projections

"We should get PC-like revenue and profit margins from mobile phones." Ma Bell, officially the American Telephone & Telegraph Co. (AT&T), had a monopoly on US telephone service until it was broken up by the US government in 1984. That spawned a "baby boom" of new telephone companies, all hungry for a share of the fast-growing long-distance phone market. That market-share hunger only intensified in the mobile phone market. Mobile technology had existed for decades, but AT&T never developed it. After the new phone companies came into existence, they invested in innovation as a fast track to increased market share. AT&T never needed to worry about market share, which stifled their need for innovation. The mobile phone market became fiercely competitive, and within a decade, these new players had created and implemented mobile phone tech on a global scale.

Extensive competition in any industry drives prices down significantly, which is great for the consumers but, in this case, was not so good for chip vendors' profits. In fact, the distribution of the cost—we call it "share of wallet"—is different when comparing mobile phones to PCs. The personal computing market evolved in such a way where Intel and AMD have dominant positions in the PC market and therefore are able to get a bigger share of wallet, resulting in high margins. This is not the case in the mobile phone market, and Intel had a hard time accepting this.

Third, Old-School Thinking

"The R&D and manufacturing methodologies, architectures, and technologies that worked in PCs and servers will work in mobile phones." No. Intel's design, development, and manufacturing process for chips was too slow, too complex, and too dependent on numerous groups and technologies. As I mentioned, some Intel POPs required several years to complete. The mobile phone market made significant progress from generation to generation every year, so faster product definition and execution methodologies were a must.

Penwell failed to meet Intel's expectations because it was designed for a market that had already moved on. I should note that the market for Penwell did not cease to exist, but the competitors had already developed better products. When Penwell was launched to market, after a two-year delay due to execution issues, it was not a competitive product. Moreover, that delay allowed another ecosystem, called ARM, to flourish in the mobile market, with companies like Qualcomm, Samsung, and Apple, which dominate the smartphone market to this day.

Continuity Is Important

One more thought on big organizations: Among business proverbs, we find, "The best way to earn a promotion is to train your successor."

Good advice. An important part of any job is mentoring what American sports teams call "the bench"—second-string players who can take over if your stars get hurt or have a bad day. In business, that's people who can replace you when you move to your next chapter.

During my last few months of leading ATOM™ CPU and SoC strategic planning, I handed off my SoC responsibilities to Itay Cohen and my ATOM™ CPU responsibilities to Alon Sella (both experienced strategic planners), and I helped them become effective in their new roles.

I did that through on-the-job training (OJT), very much like the old apprenticeship situation where an experienced craftsman worked with students to learn by doing. Sometimes it's days, sometimes weeks, sometimes months, depending on the situation.

In the beginning, they watch very closely everything you do, then, slowly, they take the lead on things to be done as you watch them, give advice, and steer them in the right direction. You teach them the vision, strategy, orchestration of tasks, connecting people involved, and all that. At some point, you move from the driver's seat to the passenger seat, so they're doing it all, coming to you only when they have specific questions. You continue guiding, but not doing. You support, encourage, empower, ask the right questions so they can figure out the answers themselves and gain confidence that they can do it on their own.

You keep this up until a) they know what to do, b) you know they know what to do, and c) they know that they know what to do. It's definitely not easy because giving control to someone else means you have to trust them with "your baby." Eventually, however, it becomes clear that you're not needed anymore. This is when you know that you're done. This is when you've freed up yourself to move higher.

Chapter 6

⚜

Reaching for the Skylake

The People

Skylake was, by far, the biggest project of my career. Skylake was Intel's sixth generation CORE™ product line. During 2008, while doing ATOM™ strategic planning, I joined the Skylake POP L0 team led by my friend and colleague, Yosi Govezensky, who later became a co-founding partner at NextLeap Ventures. I then took over as Skylake's lead strategic planner, taking it through POP L1 and POP L2 phases from 2009 to 2011. These were three very intense years where I had to build and maintain many bridges. It was a great learning experience for me. Skylake was launched to the market in early 2015 and, over its first two years, generated more than $30 billion for Intel.

That's $30 billion more money than the gross domestic product of half the nations in the world!

I did not do this alone. My main "partner in crime" was Yoav Hochberg—my friend, my boss at the time, and later a co-founding partner at NextLeap Ventures. Yoav was the vice president leading the strategic planning and business development team responsible for defining the Intel products that generated most of the revenue for the company from 2004 to 2016. He was not just my manager; he was also my guide and mentor.

I collaborated with many domain-specific strategic planners: Igal Iancu and Yuval Yosef handled perceptual computing. Maggie Auerbach handled graphics. Zach Hamm handled media and display. Gal Chanoch handled security. Yoav Talgam handled vector processing. Yosi Govezensky handled software. Rachel Moffie-Avitsur and Dror Kidron handled finance. Many others contributed, too many to name them all here.

I collaborated with many senior architects and engineering managers: Ofri Wechsler and Opher Kahn were the chief architects and Intel Fellows. Rony Friedman and Shlomit Weiss were the senior vice presidents leading the engineering. Again, many others participated.

In addition, I collaborated with the strategic planning managers of the different business groups: VP Sanjay Vora, David Knudsen, and Jon Zapp were from the Personal Computing Client Group (PCCG) strategic planning team. VP Tom Garrison and Willem Wery represented the Data Center Computing Group (DCG) strategic planning team. The senior executives who led the business units and were responsible for the multibillion-dollar P&L of their business included Mooly Eden, senior VP who led the PCCG, and Kirk Skaugen, senior VP, who led the DCG.

Finally, the ultimate decision maker for Skylake was Dadi Perlmutter, executive VP and chief product officer of Intel, who is sometimes considered the highest-ranking Israeli in the history of the global high-tech ecosystem. Dadi later joined the strategic advisory board of NextLeap Ventures—more on that to come.

During my last six months leading the Skylake strategic planning, I started handing-off my responsibilities to Yehuda Nissan, a new strategic planner that I mentored and helped him lead the POP L3 of Skylake to successful completion.

I haven't yet stated this because it should be pretty obvious, and it's the reason I've listed the names of many of my collaborators: Most of the bridges to success I've built or seen have been among people. We talk about "bridges from the present to the future" but of course, the future of the company or of society means nothing more than the future of the people employed by the company and those who live in the society. Thomas Jefferson, the third president of the United States, wrote in his retirement speech:

"The care of human life and happiness, and not their destruction, is the first and only legitimate object of good government."[9]

That was why I chose the civilian high-tech industry as my career track. I wanted to improve the happiness, morale (one might also say "hopefulness"), and well-being of people.

I also mention these people to thank them. To describe all that I learned from these people would be a book much larger than this one. That's another point which can't be stressed too enthusiastically: When you build bridges to leadership, you must build them to learn from others as well as to teach or train others to become leaders themselves. As Jack Welch, longtime chairman and CEO of General Electric (GE) wrote:

---

[9] Thomas Jefferson, *The Papers of Thomas Jefferson: Retirement Series*, ed. J. Jefferson Looney, 4 March 1809 to 15 November 1809, vol. 1 (New Jersey: Princeton University Press, 2004), 98–99.

"Before you are a leader, success is all about growing yourself. After you become a leader, success is about growing others."[10]

Let me highlight one example of real management talent: Rony Friedman was a very experienced R&D executive. He could capably manage thousands of people. He's an extremely smart person. He knows how to ask the right questions, and he knows the names and can talk with—I don't think I'm exaggerating—70 or 80 percent of all those thousands of people. Rony did all that in a way that didn't bypass the middle managers working with him. (In MNCs, there can be several layers of middle management in between the lead manager and the actual engineers working "in the trenches.") He could converse with people at all levels of the organization without anybody in the "chain of command" feeling that they were bypassed. It takes a lot of personal charm and charisma to do that in a way that doesn't offend anybody. These were all great lessons for me.

That said, Rony's real strength was using his communication gifts to get the real picture of what was happening. When you have an organization of thousands developing something, you sometimes don't learn everything from direct reports. There's never enough time to talk to everybody, and not everybody is focused on the same things. Because Rony formed very close, direct relationships—bridges to the far end of the organization—he could "think like a CEO." He understood the full picture in a far better way than most other people. That's what allowed him to ask the right questions at the right time of the right people. Those right questions meant we were sure that as we did

---

[10] John Francis Welch, Jr. and Suzy Welch, *Winning* (New York: HarperCollins, 2005).

things, we set achievable goals and could constantly measure our progress toward those goals and, of course, reach those goals on time and on budget.

The Right Tool Used Correctly

The R&D budget for Skylake was more than $1 billion, and many thousands of people worked on it. The overall time from conception to market launch was seven years, from 2008 to 2015. This is a huge machine made of people and equipment that can very easily become chaotic, and the strategic planner's job was to lead it in a coherent and focused manner towards a well-defined product line that meets budget and time constraints, as well as revenue and profit expectations. This required a very disciplined decision-making framework. We used RAPID® (a registered trademark of Bain & Company, Inc.) because we found it an effective management tool for complex decisions involving many stakeholders. There are five types of stakeholders, each having their own characteristics and responsibilities. For Skylake, we had the following:

Recommender

This is the individual, usually myself, responsible for defining the decision required, gathering inputs, crafting options, and making a recommendation on that decision.

Agreer

These are the general managers of the groups whose profit and loss (P&L) would be impacted by the decision—the general managers of business units responsible for driving the sales of Skylake to their respective markets and meeting profit projections.

Performer

These are the general managers of the groups responsible for performing the actions driven by the decision—architecture, design, manufacturing, and validation groups responsible for the development, manufacturing and testing of the different parts of the product.

Inputter

These are the people/groups providing data that affect the options at hand and, ultimately, the decision—people responsible for different aspects of the product lines, including architecture, design, manufacturing, validation, marketing, and others.

Decision Maker

This is the person who commits the organization to perform the actions driven by the decision and spend the money on those actions—in this case, Dadi Perlmutter.

After working with the system for some time, I concluded that RAPID works best with one recommender and one decision maker. In between, there can be any number of agreers, performers, and inputters, but the recommender and the decision maker should each be a "single throat to choke," as they say. This ensures effective ownership, responsibility, accountability, and results for the project. The RAPID methodology helped us bridge from uncertain, vague scenarios to clear, focused directions for execution.

I should also mention a maxim at Intel, "Execution is king." Strategy is useless without execution. As Sun Tzu wrote in *The Art of War*, "Strategy without execution is the slowest route to victory." At Intel, we used to joke that the strategic planners say *what needs to get done*, the architects say *how to do it*, and the designers decide *what to do*. People often said this with a smile, but many times, when you say something as if it's a joke, there's a lot of truth behind it. This "joke" actually means something. It means that the strategic planners and the architects have to think carefully about what they tell the designers to do. It has to be a good balance of value creation and execution realities; otherwise, the designers might decide to do something else.

That's the "chain of command," in a sense, because the designers are actually the ones who need to translate the architecture into actual transistors on the chip, if it's hardware, lines of code, or software. The designers are really the ones who do the actual job itself, and it's very important to walk the bridge all the way from the strategic planners through the architects to the designers while having a feedback loop that goes all the way back. The project lead needs to make sure that everybody is on the same page so things don't get lost in the translation.

Product Vision

In any program, there must be a vision for the product line that aligns everybody toward a clear set of end goals. This vision must be a written document, always crafted with Quintilian in mind:

"We should not write so that it is possible for the reader to understand us, but so that it is impossible for him to misunderstand us."[11]

It must be simple, clear, and succinct enough so that it can be understood, even memorized, by all the internal and external stakeholders—employees, contractors, customers, partners—everybody who'll be building, buying, or using the product. Within that vision, there are many details to be decided and acted on, but every detail must point toward the vision. Together with my partner, Yoav Hochberg, and with the help of many others, we defined a simple vision for Skylake: **Enjoy—Mobilize—Protect—Simplify—Server.** The first four words symbolized the main values of both the client (personal computers and workstations) and server (data center and cloud computers) product lines while the last word emphasized that the Skylake product line has an increased focus on the server product line, as data centers and cloud computing have become significantly more important for Intel and the world of computing.

We then continued and translated this to three high-level goals for the product line:

❖ **Optimized performance and power**—enabling high-end computing as well as thin and light mobile computing
❖ **Best graphics and media experience**—enabling rich 3D video and audio, as well as augmented and virtual reality

---

[11] Marcus Fabius Quintilianus, *Institutio Oratoria*, vol. 8 Ch.2, c. 95AD.

❖ **Robust security protection**—enabling personalization and collaboration while maintaining privacy and continuity

The Skylake product line targeted many different market segments—notebooks, laptops, and desktops in the home or office; servers in the data center; many embedded computing segments such as communication (telecom, networking), internet of things, and more. This vision served all those target segments; however, for each of them, there was a next-level-details document with goals specific to the segment, including usages, features, and actual specifications using the landing zone methodology.

To help people understand the vision and its implications, we did a "back to the future" stint. We started several of the POP decision-making meetings that we held in 2010 and 2011 with the headlines of the news that would be published in 2015. With these, we made it explicit for people. We described in a very short sentence what would be possible in 2015 and what would make the news because it was unique and new, because Skylake was available. For example, when we ratified the POR (plan of record) for the ultra-low-power family of Skylake products, we provided quotes of different end users that highlighted the value of Skylake for them:

Enjoy

❖ **Teenager**: "It's so cool—I can play the latest 3D games on my laptop, and they feel so real." This describes the value of the improvements we've made in graphics performance.

* **College freshman**: "I have lots of fun with my friends doing video chats with a real-life avatar." This describes the value of the video technologies we've integrated.
* **Child**: "This game knows how I feel. If I'm not scared enough, it changes to become scarier." This describes the value of the imaging technologies (enabling facial motion capture) we've integrated.

Mobilize

* **Real estate agent**: "I can use my laptop all day long, and my bag is lighter! I no longer carry the brick." This describes the value of the low-power SoC we developed and the long battery life.
* **Business executive**: "My laptop seamlessly displays high res on any display or projector with no cables." This describes the value of integrating wireless display capabilities.
* **Fashion designer**: "My new laptop is really sleek—so lightweight and thin that I sometimes don't feel it in my bag." This describes the value of the optimized lower-power, high-performance SoC we developed.

Protect

* **Self-employed**: "I feel more secure buying online or managing my bank and credit card accounts." This describes the integration of the software guard extensions (SGX), formerly known as the secure enclave.
* **IT manager**: "I sleep better and worry much less because my customer data is protected." This describes the security technologies we've integrated.

❖ **Credit card fraud officer**: "Intel security technology enables us to significantly reduce our fraud protection investments." This describes the security technologies we've integrated.

Simplify

❖ **Husband**: "I can wash dishes and browse the video news on my laptop using my voice to control it." This describes the value of low-power voice detection and echo cancellation we integrated into the product.

❖ **Software company CEO**: "Our apps are more robust and higher performance, and the time-to-market, R&D, validation, and support efforts were reduced." This describes the value of the simplification technologies we've integrated.

❖ **IT manager**: "I can provide more peripheral devices to my users reducing our cost of ownership." This describes the value of integrating many high-speed I/O into the product.

Finally, we also said: "After Skylake launch, Intel beats *Wall Street Journal*'s financial expectations." This helped drive people toward the vision and goals of Skylake. Indeed, Skylake launched in August 2015, and in 2016, Intel's revenue was $59.4 billion, up $4.0 billion from 2015's $55.4 billion—a very respectable 7 percent increase.

Moving to the next level of details, we also created spider-value diagrams that showcased the value that Skylake would provide on the top areas compared to the previous generation (which Intel called "goodness") and compared to the competition.

Next, we developed the LZs for the different families of the Skylake product line, as well as the die strategy and execution plans for both development and testing.

In parallel to all this, we always kept our head focused on the financial aspects of Skylake. Every milestone and decision always included a detailed financial analysis of the investment and cost as well as the projected revenues and profits.

The process was designed for large-scale projects, but the methodology can be adapted to work for smaller projects as well.

Design Partners Are Key

Another track I led, in parallel to the definition of Skylake and as a major source of input to the definition of Skylake, was the interaction with our design partners, both internal and external.

We had periodic visits and meetings with the key OEM customers that would be integrating Skylake into their systems: Apple, Dell, HP, Lenovo, LG, NEC, Panasonic, Samsung, and others. We traveled to their offices, had extensive meetings with them, showed them our directions, got their feedback, and fine-tuned our definition to better address their needs.

In addition, we had interactions with internal design partners. For example, to better understand the needs of a data center, we collaborated with the people who led the Intel data center, which was used for Intel's computing needs. At that time, Intel's Haifa data center was the largest in the Middle East. Given the scale and advanced computing needs of Intel's R&D organization, these data centers were using leading-edge technologies to provide the best computing experiences for Intel employees and partners. These internal Intel teams were actually the customers of Intel's customers—that is, they would buy server platforms from Dell or HP or others, companies that were buying the server chips from Intel that we were defining. I asked them to provide us with two lists:

❖ All the problems and issues they faced using Intel-based servers
❖ The features and capabilities of their "dream server"

We used these lists as a guideline for improving the definition of the Skylake server to better meet the future needs of the data center and cloud markets—another set of bridges that enabled Intel to create and capture value.

New Technologies

A big part of the Skylake product line definition included the definition of the new technologies that would be developed and integrated into the different Skylake platforms. In addition to my role as the lead strategic planner of Skylake, I also served as the lead technologies strategic planner and drove the decision making on which technologies to integrate. This was a highly complex task that involved many stakeholders across many organizations at Intel. In other programs, the lead strategic planner and the lead technologies strategic planner were two different individuals; however, I felt that the outcome would be better if I took both roles.

We started with proposals for integrating more than forty different technologies and ended up adding only twenty-one technologies to the POR for Skylake. This was the bridge between "wishful thinking" (*what we'd like to do* to increase the value that Skylake delivers to the different stakeholders) and "reality" (*what is feasible* from the execution, cost, and risk perspectives).

You may ask yourself, how did I do it? We formed a multidisciplinary team of thirty-eight experts. It included myself, representatives from fourteen different groups—composed of eight technology groups plus six business units (a strategic planner and an architect from each)—and nine strategic planners who represented the different domains of Skylake. This team evaluated the technologies and came up with a recommendation to the POP team of the technologies that would provide the highest return on investment (ROI). All this had to be aligned to the Skylake vision and goals.

The process had to be well-organized and very disciplined since it included so many stakeholders, opinions, and interests, plus a huge amount of data. It was important to prioritize technologies in a streamlined process (involving all stakeholders) to reach a balanced mix of value and risk, and as we learned in smartphones, we had to do it before the market simply passed our products by.

The first thing I did (which I learned from Yoav Talgam, who led technologies strategic planning in prior programs) was develop a *technology score card*, a template for each technology proposed that included

- ❖ the highlights of its value, maturity, and enabling it would require;
- ❖ the impact on other parts of the platform;
- ❖ the investment required to implement it; and
- ❖ the proposed plan and risk mitigation strategy.

Each technology owner had to fill the scorecard and present it to the working group. They got feedback from the team, then improved their analysis of the technology in terms of value provided and investment required, and updated their scorecard. After several months of this back and forth, we held a three-day face-to-face meeting of the entire working group where technology owners presented their technologies again (with their refined strategy and action plan) to the whole team. Toward the end of the face-to-face workshop, we held a prioritization session where each of the business unit representatives provided a rating and ranking on each technology for their target market.

The business units represented notebooks, desktops, servers, embedded graphics, and software. I then compiled the whole list, giving different weights to the ratings of the different business units according to their importance—notebooks, desktops, and servers had highest impact on the list because those business units drove the largest share of revenue and profit. The results of the face-to-face workshop, for example, the list of technologies for path finding, were then presented to the POP team and approved by it.

After this, the architecture team conducted path finding on the technologies and provided their assessment of the feasibility of each, given available resources, expertise, and constraints. Their response was used to re-evaluate the prioritized technologies list. Finally, we came to an agreed-upon list of prioritized technologies that we brought to the POP team for approval. It was later brought to the POP L2 decision meeting to approve that list of technologies for the POR. In each of these steps, the RAPID model ensured clear and effective progress toward a coherent, feasible set of technologies that would create and capture value.

Lessons for Leading Big Teams

In leading big teams, the bridge to success requires a well-structured methodology to ensure effectiveness and efficiency. (Structure is also valuable in small projects, but in those, more flexibility is possible, simply because there are fewer bodies involved.) Big teams include many people with different skill sets, experiences, values, goals, and characteristics. The leader must be able to "herd the cats" and align everybody on the convergent path that leads to the vision via completion of the goals or leads to the shutdown of the program or group because the project is determined to be unworkable. The mechanics of this starts with the formation of a working group (WG):

❖ Which stakeholders do you need to define the vision and goals and translate them to a plan of action?
❖ It's important to include all the key people (or their representatives) that you envision would be on the RAPID model for what you're trying to accomplish.
❖ In most matrix organizations, these stakeholders are not part of the leader's group, so the leader does not manage them directly.
❖ The leader needs to develop a relationship with them that would allow him/her to direct the stakeholders to do what is needed to advance the group to the successful completion of its goals.

I've found the most effective way to operate such a group includes a weekly (sometimes more frequent) recurring meeting with all the stakeholders. These recurring meetings must be on everybody's calendars in a regular, scheduled slot. (For Skylake, this meant two hours every Thursday, at a time convenient for people on the US' West Coast and in Israel.)

Keep these meetings going. Cancellation or postponement should only be when necessary. "Necessary" and "convenient" are very different things, by the way! The leader must ensure that the wheels are in motion all the time in order to make real progress. To do this requires the following:

- ❖ The working group must understand that this meeting is the priority. They have to schedule their other activities around the weekly WG meetings. They are periodic, and they never move or cancel unless there's a real emergency (not a perceived one). This is critical to the effectiveness of the WG. I'll say it again—the meetings don't move and are not cancelled unless there's a real emergency.
- ❖ Practice management-by-presentation as outlined in Chapter 1, under "How Start-ups Are Successful," to enable holistic yet detailed progress.
- ❖ Don't plan each meeting individually. Plan a coherent agenda for meetings over the succeeding five to ten weeks, updating that plan as needed.
- ❖ Publish that schedule to all stakeholders with the minutes you write up after every session.
- ❖ Each agenda should include each topic and owner presenting. (Don't put an owner on the agenda to present a topic before the owner accepts that task.)

❖ Work behind the scenes with topic owners, defining their topics of responsibility and presentation schedule.

❖ Book a presentation only when it fits the overall progress of the program to ensure you can meet the goals and milestones.

❖ A few days before each meeting, publish the agenda, including topics and owners. Review with the owners the content each will present to ensure the right content comes to the meeting. (Such preparation is crucial to ensure that the actual meeting is effective, and people feel they're part of a professional working group that's doing things right.)

❖ During the meeting, steer the discussion toward achieving concrete decisions and specific action items as the next steps.

❖ After the meeting, publish the minutes, also described in Chapter 1, under "How Start-ups Are Successful."

Weekly meetings can be held in person if everyone is in the same building or city. Increasingly, especially when dealing with larger projects in larger companies, meetings are virtual, via video or audio link. (For us at Intel and in other multinational corporations, this has been the norm for many decades.) In addition, I think it is critical, in most cases to schedule quarterly face-to-face meetings, typically one or two days, in which the decisions are made and the major milestones are reviewed and approved.

Communication is the key to aligning many stake-holders on a convergent path to achieving the goals that will realize the vision. Once again, I note that humans are, by nature, separated by gaps of experience, skill sets, and goals. Each of us naturally focuses on tactical and personal goals (for ourselves or our team or department) while strategic successes require "CEO-like" vision that bridges all the teams and departments, creating a path, or perhaps a highway, that accomplishes the vision. The excellence exhibited in the leader's work ethic will be reflected in the work ethic of team members. As the working group's facilitator, the team lead ensures clear communication—the holistic, big-picture view that sees both the trees *and* the forest.

The lead balances strategic discussions and tactical discussions—both are equally needed. The lead ensures all stakeholders are heard respectfully, that debates are focused on data and content and not on personal rivalries. Ego is a fundamental aspect of every person, and discussions can sometimes become quite heated. The leader must calmly bring the discussion back to the envisioned path. To summarize, in every meeting, from the weekly conference call to the quarterly face-to-face, the team lead must do all these:

- ❖ Set clear objectives and milestones.
- ❖ Identify key individuals and become their friend.
- ❖ Practice Manage-by-Presentations.
- ❖ Conduct one-on-one pre-meetings with presenters for dry runs and buy-ins.
- ❖ Don't be afraid to ask tough questions.
- ❖ Publish a clear agenda before the meeting, with topics, presenters, and times.
- ❖ Publish succinct minutes after the meeting, with an executive summary and detailed notes highlighted as appropriate.

❖ Communicate (verbally and in minutes) all decisions and action items.

Discipline and order—"keeping your eyes on the prize," in common jargon—keeps the team moving forward in its most efficient and effective manner.

Chapter 7

⬱

A Strategic Outlook Leads Disruptive Innovation

Development of the Skylake project began in 2008, and the product came to market in 2015. That's many millions of labor hours spread over seven calendar years. If a company is to make such an investment of time, effort, money, and other resources, it has to expect a substantial return on that investment. To earn that return, companies must have a sweeping strategy. They must take a very long-term view of things, building the ultimate bridge between present and future.

I once heard of a large business owner who planned for his company's next three hundred years. Given the changes of the last three centuries, I don't recommend planning that farsighted in most cases. There are practical limits to our predictive ability. (Still, such forethought is impressive.)

To ensure that a product line includes the right technologies and enables the required usages for the time of its launch to the market, enabling it to be a winning product, we developed the Long-Term Outlook.

What Is a Long-Term Outlook?

My last five years at Intel were focused on disruptive innovation, as I led the Strategic Technologies Group. The strategic planning organization must figure out these:

❖ What is it that users (corporate and consumer) will need or want three to six years from now?
❖ What products will meet those needs and wants profitably?

Thus, the Long-Term Outlook (LTO) was developed, which is, in a nutshell, envisioning the future, analyzing the ecosystem, predicting how it will move forward, describing what the world might look like in half a decade to a decade, and devising a strategy to meet the needs of that forecasted future.

"Strategy" has a lot of definitions, and different people have different views on it, but one thing is certain: strategy is useless if you don't know where you want to get to. LTO is about defining that "where to." It is a holistic process that stretches the following:

❖ "Inside out" because it includes the internal experts' view of where the world is going
❖ "Outside in" because it includes the external experts' view of where the world is going
❖ "Top down" since it includes an understanding of humans needs, aspirations and challenges
❖ "Bottom up" since it includes an understanding of the latest and expected technological advancements in academia, start-ups, and corporations

The metaphor I like to use is the iceberg: 10 percent is visible above the surface of the water, the rest below. The LTO is a comprehensive body of work with a key executive summary that is "visible above the water," a matrix of two dimensions:

- ❖ **Mega-themes**. These are the paradigm shifts and the major trends and transformations expected to occur during the next ten years—those innovations that matter most because they have the biggest impact. This part of the document describes the usages, capabilities, technologies, and forces delivering a meaningful paradigm shift that will drive the digital and physical ecosystems. We also provided proof points that are happening today and trigger events that may drive disruptive innovation for each theme.
- ❖ **Verticals**. These are the different industrial sectors—i.e., transportation, healthcare, manufacturing, government, entertainment, education, and so on. Here we describe how each of these sectors may be impacted by each mega theme or combination of mega themes.

Why LTO?

The LTO serves as a backdrop for creating strategies, determining goals to achieve, and directions to follow. It is another bridge between the present and the future. While I was at Intel, we used the LTO as the beacon or lighthouse. For example, if *this* is where the world is going (according to the LTO) and I am the client computing group, then I need to develop *these* strategies and products.

My group translated the LTO into technologies and came up with a list of more than a hundred technology domains that need to exist and develop in order for the LTO predictions to be realized within the next ten years. Then we would take this list, evaluate, and set priorities in terms of two main elements:

- ❖ How important is it from a business and impact perspective? How transformative and disruptive will it be to existing or new markets?
- ❖ How important is it for Intel to develop a *sustainable strategic advantage* in this technology domain? How easy is it for Intel, given our history and desired future to lead the cutting edge of this domain?

How to Develop the LTO

Developing the LTO is a big project that requires multidisciplinary knowledge and expertise. Yosi Govezensky was on the team and took responsibility for driving the LTO. Yosi gathered a cross-organization team of experts from many different Intel groups—client business, server business, Intel Labs (the research organization), sales and marketing, engineering, finance, among others. Some of these experts were business-focused, some were user-experience-focused, some were market-research-focused, and some were technology-focused. We needed to combine all these disciplines and develop a unified view of where the world would probably go.

We had a remote virtual weekly meeting plus face-to-face quarterly meetings lasting several days, where we brainstormed on different scenarios and developed a coherent view of the world's future. We acted in close collaboration with David Ginsberg, Intel's chief strategy officer (CSO) and his team, as well as with Intel Futurists Brian David Johnson and Steve Brown.

The sources or inputs to the LTO need to be broad and deep. They included demographic trends, futurists' analysis, market research, technology road maps, and much more. They even included science fiction books and movies! I envisioned all these inputs as "whispers from the future." We gathered all of them and tried to figure out which are more important than the others. Since there are so many inputs and they are many times obscured, it's like finding a needle in a haystack and separating the wheat from the chaff—both done hundreds or thousands of times.

We used many tools and methodologies to develop the LTO, for example, future casting and back casting, S-curve analysis, canvasing, black swan, scenario planning, and more. One methodology I particularly liked was the usages face-to-face workshop. This started with Intel ethnographers' and sociologists' descriptions of ten personas. Each persona was a real person—that is, a seventy-year-old retired English schoolteacher (female); an eight-year-old boy from Portland, Oregon; a fifteen-year-old Brazilian high school student (female); a thirty-five-year-old Korean businesswoman; a forty-five-year-old financial industry professional from New York; a thirty-year-old female French graphic designer; and others.

The team would follow them for weeks, interviewing them about their needs, problems, fears, and aspirations, in general and with respect to technology. We would hold a two-to-three-day face-to-face meeting with all relevant stakeholders, and the personas were introduced to us using movies, graphs, and text. Then we split into roundtables of multidisciplinary groups, each focused on a single persona, and brainstormed about potential usages, capabilities, and systems that the specific persona would use/have in ten years. After a few hours, each table would present their work to the whole group. The combined thinking of these people, focusing on different potential users, gave us a good overview of the possibilities. It was one set of the bricks (out of many) for the bridge we were building between the present and the future, in the framework of the LTO.

Like the work I described on Skylake Technologies, here as well, we developed a template for the mega themes in the LTO. This included several key areas:

❖ **Mega theme name**. The name must encompass the essence of the thing in one to three words.
❖ **Description**. The description should tell the reader what this is about in one to two sentences.
❖ **Paradigm shifts**. The key fundamental changes that may happen in this area changes in basic assumptions: if you could be in the future, and somebody asked you, "what has changed?" what would you answer?
❖ **End point**. This is the list of attributes, capabilities, characteristics, insights, or technologies that enrich the definition of the theme.
❖ **Indicators**. Assuming the end point, what are the key business, usage, technology enablers, and technology inhibitors, in the short term, the medium term, and the long term?

❖ **Trigger**. This is a single episode that is substantial and has an irreversible impact; it causes a nonlinear acceleration of the mega theme.
❖ **Examples of usages**. These are examples of potential usages describing the values and benefits of the area.
❖ **Potential technology impact**. This is a partial list of technologies related to the mega theme.

Once the work on the mega themes reached a decent level of maturity, we would start developing the vertical industries perspectives. The verticals themselves changed over the years, but they typically included the following: defense, education, entertainment (including gaming, sports, and arts), financials, government, health care, law enforcement, manufacturing, retail, transportation, and utilities. For each of these verticals, we would show how each of the mega themes impacted them and what potential usages would emerge.

Geographical Perspectives

When we did the LTO for the first several years, we had a unified worldwide view that did not pay too much attention to geography. During 2014, we reconsidered the LTO and concluded that the unified worldwide view was no longer valid. We needed to augment it with a focused view on China (and later, perhaps, also on India), which started our annual visits to China in 2015. Together with the Intel China Strategy Office, we developed an LTO for China that was included in (and influenced) the global LTO. China has had the world's largest population for centuries and, therefore, has been a big market for

Intel and other companies. Throughout the years, China became the main source of mass-produced goods, most of which were designed and developed in other countries.

From an LTO perspective, most of China's influence was, in the past, on China itself, but during the early years of the twenty-first century, China increased its innovation prowess and started impacting the world outside its borders. That's why we saw the need for a focused LTO. A top-tier example is WeChat—a Chinese instant messaging, social media, and mobile payment app developed by Tencent. First released in 2011, it became the world's largest standalone mobile app in 2018, with over one billion monthly active users, and it had a big impact, directly and indirectly, on a worldwide scale.

We came to understand that many times, a one-size-fits-all strategy or framework doesn't work well. One must consider the different geographical perspectives and fine-tune the vision, strategy, tactics, plans, and actions to the different countries around the world.

LTO Lives On

In 2016, I hired Nitai Friedman to lead the LTO when Yosi Govezensky left Intel. Three years later (two years after I left Intel), Nitai called and asked us, the NextLeap Ventures co-founding partners—Yosi Govezensky, Yoav Hochberg, Ronny Korner, Ido Lapidot, and myself—to develop a new LTO for Intel, this time as external subcontractors. Since NextLeap Ventures was using the LTO framework to help identify and select the most promising start-ups for investment, we did not lose this "muscle" of doing the Long-Term Outlook. We were happy to have Intel pay us to do this work for them. We used the tools and methodologies described earlier and came up with the following mega themes—in alphabetical order:

- ❖ **A picture is worth a thousand words**. Video and visuals become the basic information method for communication.
- ❖ **Autonomous everything**. All devices will include a form of autonomous capability with varying degrees of intelligence, some fully and some partially autonomous.
- ❖ **Body and soul**. Increasing leisure time and putting a higher focus on well-being, sports, and e-sports (a space that is rising) represent a shift in how much and how people spend their scarcest resource— time; gaming becomes no longer just a game.
- ❖ **Digital disruption maturing**. Legacy verticals will go end to end digital, disrupting every industry.
- ❖ **E-mperium**. This is digital disruption of governments and governance:
  - o Technology impacts governments and regulations.
  - o Companies become as large and influential as countries (companies like Amazon, Apple, Face-book, and Google).
- ❖ **Intelligent digital mesh**. All devices seamlessly connected in a network, sharing data, insights, resources, and working coherently to solve problems; all mirrored in the virtual space.
- ❖ **Living data**. Data is perceived and handled as a biological entity.
- ❖ **Resource scarcity and saving the world**. Using technology to manage every resource; sustainability

becomes a driving force rather than just an afterthought.

❖ **Space, the next frontier**. Humanity expands to harsh environments, the oceans then outer space, to address the needs of the growing world population.

❖ **Super humans**
   o Hunters and gatherers deal with technology—the interaction and impact of new technology on humanity, as individuals and as a society
   o Augmented self—living longer, healthier with improved capabilities
   o Cyber-physical humans (as in the television show *The Bionic Man*)—the merge of technology and humanity to build something new

After several months of work, we presented the LTO to a group of a few dozen of Intel VPs as part of the kick-off of Intel's 2020 strategic long-range planning (SLRP). It's pretty amazing that although more than two years passed since I left Intel, I still had an impact (together with my friends and partners) on Intel's strategic directions. Moreover, the LTO continues to be an integral and important part of the NextLeap Ventures methodology for selecting promising start-ups for investment, and it also helps us in guiding and supporting our portfolio companies as they develop their strategies.

Intrapreneurship

Long Lead Technologies

Intrapreneurship is the bridge between disruptive innovation and multinational corporations. While at Intel, one of our guiding frameworks was called long lead technology (LLT). These are transformational technology areas driven by the LTO.

They

* have potential for creating *sustainable strategic advantages*, enabling the company to differentiate and win in the marketplace in the mid to long term;
* are aligned to the company's long-term outlook;
* are transformative or disruptive, creating new value that can be monetized to deliver significant revenue and profit;
* require long development cycles but with line of sight for solution, and the technology is mature enough to have moved from academia/theory to the commercial/practical sector, yet significant development is still required to make it commercially available for mass markets; and
* are not currently "funded for success" within the company.

In a nutshell, LLTs are the technologies that will meet the future predicted by the LTO.

Identifying LLTs

Having established the LTO, the LLT identification phase starts with decomposing the LTO into technology domains. If the world will look as we envision it, then what technologies will enable that vision to become reality?

This decomposition resulted in a long list of over 100 technology domains. Not all of them are new, and not all of them are transformational or disruptive. So one must screen, filter, aggregate, and prioritize the domains using the criteria above. The technologies are reviewed repeatedly vis-à-vis the criteria, each phase reducing the number of LLT candidates.

For example, when we did this in 2014, we started with 188 technology domains. After careful review, we selected the top 26 candidates. We then reviewed them against the criteria, selecting the top 11 candidates. As a final step, we did pair-wise comparisons of the top candidates across all criteria and all possible pairs of candidates and came up with the top 3 domains:

- ❖ **Audio understanding**—including natural language understanding
- ❖ **Brain-inspired Hardware**—later called neuromorphic computing
- ❖ **Pico systems**—tiny systems with sub-millimeter dimensions

This process may seem overly complex, but remember, the monetary investment will be huge, and the development to market will require years, so the task of selecting the top LLTs has to be rigorous and exhaustive, and to put it mildly, sometimes, it's also exhausting.

Additionally, you can challenge the process by coming up with "wild cards," which are domains that didn't meet the criteria as well as the others, but you put them on the list anyway. In 2014, we collectively decided that we needed to add another 2 domains as wild cards:

- ❖ **Crypto currencies and digital ledger**—for example, blockchain, as a means for distributed secure value exchange and Bitcoin (or another crypto currency) as a digital currency without a central banking system

❖ **Programmable science**—the convergence of digital, biological, and chemical worlds, delivering new, hybrid solutions providing significantly higher value than using any of these domains alone

In 2012, my first year leading the strategic technologies group, we identified a different set of LLTs and got another new set each year since. How often should you define your new LLTs is a question that depends on the type and size of your organization.

Incubation of LLTs

Following the identification of an LLT domain, an owner is assigned to it, and he or she becomes the intrapreneur responsible for driving this domain into the company. A typical incubation of an LLT lasts one to three years. In this incubation phase, we focus on all aspects of the technology domain, including architectures, business models, technologies, usage models, and much more. We build a bridge from vision/concept to executable plans (technologies and products) for making such vision/concepts a reality within a reasonably short period. These bridges help us define the means of creating and capturing value within that specific LLT domain.

I had several intrapreneurs in my team—some reported to me, and some were "dotted line"—who led the incubation of specific LLTs over the years. Many of them became good friends of mine, including Ido Lapidot, who later became a co-founding partner in

NextLeap Ventures. Ido taught us the method of TRIZ[12] (theory of inventive problem solving) used to solve hard problems and predict evolution of technologies and products. We used it regularly as part of the LTO and the LLTs incubation. We continue to use TRIZ at NextLeap Ventures to help us predict the probability of success of start-ups that we evaluate for investment. We also use it to help our portfolio companies create and execute a compelling road map of technologies and products.

Intrapreneurship is similar to establishing a new start-up, except that it's done within the boundaries and constraints of a large corporation. Therefore, an important part of incubation includes the organizational aspects since we need to find a way to drive this LLT domain into the POR. Graduation of the LLT incubation requires that

- ❖ the right executive must take ownership of the execution plan for the specific domain;
- ❖ a business unit must say, "I want this because it helps my unit's profitability."; and
- ❖ an engineering group must say, "I know how to develop this technology and deliver a *sustainable strategic advantage.*"

Sometimes these groups don't exist, and they have to be created. Once these elements are in place, the LLT, as we said, "has graduated" to become part of the POR.

LLT incubation can take different shapes and forms, as not all LLTs are created equal. Nevertheless, together with one of my intrapreneurs, Ariel Moshkovitz, who

---

[12] TRIZ: https://en.wikipedia.org/wiki/TRIZ

continues to be a good friend of mine, we developed a framework to address the general aspects of incubating an LLT towards successful graduation.

The framework aims to better ensure credible and effective LLT execution while providing the needed autonomy for long-lead technology incubation such that innovation is not constrained and the direction that will provide the best ROI is followed. The framework defines the life cycle of the LLT incubation—the activities, deliverables, and the decision-making process and owners. The objectives of the LLT incubation framework are the following:

❖ Enable effective execution of LLT incubation, optimizing time and resources.
❖ Enable the highest possible probability for successful graduation.
❖ Provide transparency to management while maintaining team autonomy.
❖ Be flexible and dynamic while delivering expected outcomes.
❖ Provide constant feedback and meet validation checkpoints.
❖ Ensure each phase challenges the key questions and deliverables.

The five phases of the framework are the following:

❖ **Discovery**—market/ecosystem, academia, and internal scan and analysis; development of usages; assembling the incubation team
❖ **Strategy formulation**—development of vision and strategy; identification of possible technologies, partners, business models, business units, and proof of concept (POC) opportunities

❖ **Planning**—developing the road map and milestones towards POC-IP-technology
❖ **Execution**—project execution and handover options evaluation
❖ **Transfer**—handover to the engineering and business unit groups, including collateral and knowledge transfer

At the end of each phase, there is a decision meeting where the outcome of the phase is presented and discussed, and a decision is made to a) continue to the next phase, b) stop working on the LLT, or c) continue with the current phase to complete missing information, which will require another decision meeting before moving to the next phase.

Discovery typically takes one to three months and includes these:

❖ Initial business analysis—problem statement and background, relevance to Intel, initial market-academy Intel scan
❖ Initial technologies analysis—existing technologies and solutions
❖ Initial usages analysis
❖ LLT team assembly
❖ Initial definition of LLT plan

Strategy Formulation typically takes another one to three months and includes these:

❖ Define LLT strategy—vision, Intel value proposition, identify possible POCs and collaborations
❖ Needed/enabling technologies identified

❖ Relevant external/internal partners identified

Planning typically takes another one to three months and includes these:

❖ Define LLT road map and deliverables—POC, IP/ technologies
❖ Ask for funding and other resources to support the road map
❖ Final business case, including market, financial, usage, and technology analyses
❖ Initial IP/technologies proposal—that is, the initial LZ
❖ LLT execution plan

Execution can take from three to eighteen months and includes these:

❖ POC deliverables
❖ IP/technologies deliverables—LZ and high-level architecture
❖ Handoff road map—options and stakeholders
❖ Schedule

Throughout the whole incubation in all phases, the LLT incubation team and the intrapreneur should also focus on the following:

❖ Key questions, objectives, and technologies challenged and rephrased as part of each phase deliverables
❖ Patent filing
❖ Lessons learned and retrospective

Those key questions, which the intrapreneur and team must keep in mind at all times, include the following:

- ❖ What's the relevance to specific engineering and/or business unit and potential IPs?
- ❖ What's the relevance to Intel?
- ❖ Does the action support the LLT objectives?
- ❖ Do we have the right partner(s), internally and or externally, to achieve the objectives?
- ❖ What is the potential market value?
- ❖ What are the differentiation/innovative factors?
- ❖ Are we addressing a critical pain point?
- ❖ Are we enabling new, compelling usages?

Transfer typically takes one to three months and includes these:

- ❖ Deliver all required documentation
- ❖ Transfer all technical and business deliverables

Following the conclusion of the transfer, we would kick off a retrospective of the LLT incubation to learn and improve our methodology.

Seem complex and exhaustive? It is, and it is so by design. I repeat from earlier in this chapter: If a company is to make a major investment of time, effort, money, and other resources, it has to expect a substantial return on that investment. To earn that return, companies must have a sweeping strategy—they must take a very long-term view of things. And I add that this detailed and complex process minimizes the chances of failure. An old sage once said, "History is the proof of the theory." This process was extensively tested at Intel, and it proved its worth in ensuring successful graduation of numerous LLT domains.

Case Study: Computer Vision and Machine Learning

Back in 2012, computer vision and machine learning (important parts of AI—artificial intelligence) was an LLT we identified, and Oren Gershon of my team was the intrapreneur responsible for driving it. This is probably the most successful LLT incubation we did during my time with the Intel Strategic Technologies Group.

We identified it as an LLT following the LTO of 2011 when we realized that most of the information humans get on the world is visual, and we saw significant progress in the technologies (hardware, software, algorithms) that started showing a line of sight to commercial machines that can learn, see, and understand what they see. In 2012, it became clear this was a disruptive domain just starting to mature towards commercialization. The 2012 ImageNet Challenge had just shown a significant improvement in the ability of neural networks to perform computer vision tasks. *The Economist* said of this, "Suddenly people started to pay attention, not just within the AI community but across the technology industry as a whole."[13]

At the time, we called this LLT "visual understanding," and we convinced the architecture team to assign a group of senior architects and software engineers to develop prototypes for computer vision. The group was

---

[13] The Economist, "From Not Working to Neural Networking," The Economist (The Economist Newspaper Limited, June 23, 2016), https://www.economist.com/special-report/2016/06/23/from-not-working-to-neural-networking.

led by Roman Fishtein and included Sergey Gofman, Rinat Rappoport, Boaz Tamir, and others. With them and under the leadership of Oren Gershon, we defined and developed a prototype showcasing many visual understanding usages and technologies. During 2013, we managed to convince Rony Friedman (then-Intel corporate vice president) to establish the Computer Vision Group (CVG), and Oren Gershon moved from my team to lead the strategic planning of the CVG.

One of my favorite activities that we did as part of the incubation of visual understanding, in 2012, was an interactive crowd ideation contest, which was led by Ronny Korner, my friend, our group's business development person and later a co-founding partner of NextLeap Ventures. We partnered with an external agency and published the following challenge/contest:

Imagine five years into the future...

You have on you (or with you) a new sensing technology that can see, hear, remember, and understand everything around you all the time.

What would you do with it? What would it look like?

We asked people, across the globe to submit ideas in the form of text, drawings, and illustrations, and we received 488 idea submissions from 449 people. These people came from eighty-seven nations, yet two countries stood out—Israel and India. Many of the ideas came from these two countries. Our judges selected the three winners of the contest (without knowing who they were and where they come from)—two Israelis and one Indian. One of the winners was particularly interesting: They called it The Intel Soulmate, and it included a ring for your finger used to control glasses that include audio and visual inputs/outputs. They provided a nice description of how the system tracks, records, reminds, captures, keeps, retrieves, and assists the user with all daily life activities.

During 2014, together with Igal Iancu, from the Perceptual Computing Group (PCG), Yoram Zahavi, the intrapreneur who led cognitive computing (CC) in my team, and Gadi Singer, the general manager of the architecture team, we developed a strategic business plan for Intel to double-down on machine learning, cognitive computing, and computer vision. The business plan was presented to Mooly Eden, then-president of Intel Israel and GM of PCG. He pitched it to Renee James, then-president of Intel.

This was a seminal document, with input from many Intel experts, describing the vision, strategy, and action plan for Intel to become the world leader in computer vision, cognitive computing, and machine learning. The investment required would be a few hundred million dollars. Unfortunately, our proposal was not approved and were not funded. Instead, under the umbrella of Rony Friedman, and the leadership of Ofri Wechsler, the CVG continued to grow in size and capability and included several dozen engineers focused on developing computer vision and machine-learning hardware and software. These were integrated into Intel's road map of products. When Intel formed its Artificial Intelligence Platform Group (AIPG) following the acquisition of Nervana Systems in 2016, CVG became part of Nervana, and Oren Gershon became the leader of the Computer Vision and Deep Learning Software Group.

In 2017, parts of the group that originated in our LLT (back in 2012) merged with the Mobileye team that Intel acquired that year for more than $15 billion. Oren

Gershon later became an Intel VP and now leads the development of significant products and technologies at Intel.

That's a rather long way of saying you sometimes get where you want to be via "the scenic route," not always along the path you first set out to follow. As I said before, in large corporations, there is always politics and, I would add, a variety of points-of-view in the upper echelons of management. They may know things or have priorities that you are not aware of. You have to realize that you don't always control everything when you work for a large corporation.

Patent Filing

An important aspect of LLT incubation as well as start-ups and corporate R&D is the filing of patents to guarantee creators' rights respecting intellectual property (IP). This bridge ensures the business has a secured path toward success. It protects your ability to capture value and monetize the innovations you produce. Patents focus mostly on technologies and usages, yet they serve two vital business goals:

Defense

Patents need to be filed on technologies and usages as soon as they start to form to help protect the company against potential lawsuits. Competitors may claim they developed similar inventions prior to yours. If proven that your company's technology infringed on competitor's patents, a small company can lose everything. An MNC like Intel has deep pockets, and less-than-scrupulous persons may file a nuisance lawsuit in the hope that the MNC will pay them off (even if their claim is bogus) to avoid a more-costly trial. The self-defense aspect of patents cannot be underestimated.

Offense

Filing patents on technologies and usages before you launch products to market helps the company win against competing products that emerge after you launch. Date of filing is the basis of ownership in patent law. A competitor may develop a similar tech, but if you file the patent before they do, the innovation is protected as your property. In a small start-up developing innovative solutions, a strong offence deters others. Patents are also business assets. If a larger corporation is exploring a merger-and-acquisition deal with you, patents make you more attractive and increase your valuation.

Chapter 8

ॐ

Process Makes for Progress

Leading Teams

While at Intel, I learned and implemented some of the foremost methodologies for leading teams. It's important to understand the fundamental concept of a team: It's a group of people joining forces to accomplish something none of them could accomplish on their own. Teams require synchronization and alignment among the individuals to create synergy—the idea that the whole is greater than the sum of the parts, as I described in Chapters 1 and 2, with the tale of the Belgian draft horses.

Teams must deliver results and continuously improve if they want to continue being important for their organization. In the high-pace, high-tech world we live in, it's not enough to do the same things again and again. You have to constantly reinvent yourself, deliver more results, and improve in order to stay relevant, reach a leadership position, and maintain it. To achieve those goals, you need to define objectives and metrics and measure your progress on these metrics as you progress toward delivering results.

At Intel, we used the management by objectives (MBO) system developed by Peter Drucker.[14] MBO is all about defining objectives and measuring the progress towards achieving them. When you lead a team of senior people, I recommend using the MBO methodology on a quarterly basis:

- ❖ Near the end of each quarter, you sit with your management, review the previously-defined objectives for your team, and grade your progress toward those objectives.
- ❖ You then define your team's objectives for the next quarter and approve them with your management.
- ❖ You then sit with each team member and do the same with each of them. In some teams it makes sense to do this with the whole team together, in addition, or instead of, doing it with each team member separately.
- ❖ They then do the same with the people who report to them, and so on.
- ❖ Repeat every quarter, with more focused attention at the end of each year.

The annual performance review (APR), or performance appraisal, is another important tool for managing and leading people. It typically includes three parts, and I recommend discussing three items in each part in order to be effective and succinct:

---

[14] Peter Drucker, *Practice of Management.* (New York: Harper Business, 1954).

- ❖ **Accomplishments**. These are top three results the employee achieved during the period, highlighting their impact and importance.
- ❖ **Strengths**. These are the top three characteristics the employee displayed during the period, highlighting how they helped the employee make an impact.
- ❖ **Development**. These are three areas for growth and improvement the employee should focus on during the next performance period and how these areas will help the employee grow and increase impact.

I've found great value in asking the employee to write their own performance review. The employee sends their review to the manager, who takes it as a draft, adding his/her own view of the performance. The manager and team member then meet and the manager presents what he/she wrote.

A discussion and bidirectional feedback follows.

As their manager, I always request an evaluation from my employees. I ask them, explicitly, if and how I can better help them. I make sure to end on a positive, optimistic note, highlighting the potential and the future work we can do together, to grow and achieve better and more significant results and impact.

I also use MBO and APR for the team as a unit. Synergy is the goal, and it's important to measure and reflect on how we're doing as a team: What were our objectives and how did we progress towards achieving them?

Recognizing and celebrating success is another great tool to motivate, drive growth, and improve performance of individuals and teams. I learned this very young, as I noted in Chapter 1. When key milestones are achieved, either individual or team-wide, recognize that success publicly. You may choose to celebrate them in a team lunch or some other fun, out-of-the-office event. This strengthens the bond between the team members, builds more bridges between them, and enables the team to work better as a team in the long run. For example, my team enjoyed going golfing together, hiking in the mountains of the Galilee, touring the old city of Jerusalem, and more.

Retrospective

A retrospective upon program completion (successful or unsuccessful) can be priceless. Particularly in unsuccessful projects, it isn't about blame. There's always plenty of that to go around and publicly shaming people does nothing good for company or individual morale and future productivity. In unsuccessful projects, you want to learn, improve, and grow to identify mistakes and devise ways to avoid them in the future. This works on all levels—individual, teams, and company-wide.

That old sage also said, tongue-in-cheek, "People who learn from past mistakes are freed to make all-new mistakes in the future." Be honest—no person, group, or process is perfect. Striving toward perfection is important, but usually, "Perfect is the enemy of good."

A good retrospective involves all the stakeholders, internal and external, of the project and the company. Internally, you want to interview and get the perspectives of most of the RAPID stakeholders. Externally, you want to get perspectives from several end-users, customers, partners, or investors. Each has a unique perspective, and all are valuable. You can perform the retrospective in a variety of ways—questionnaires, one-on-one interviews, group meetings, or in any way that works for you. The goal of the retrospective is gathering useful information about the project so you can learn, grow, and improve. To make retrospective an effective tool for growth and improvement, it should have three parts, noticeably similar to the APR content:

❖ **What went well**? We first focus on the positive: to reinforce the good things we did, encourage team members to continue doing them, and soften the blow of our shortcomings. Detail, as clearly as possible, what went well in the project, why it succeeded, or what positives it accomplished, even if the program failed overall.

❖ **What went wrong**? We identify the symptoms and the root cause of failure. Many times, people focus only on the symptoms (such as, "We missed this milestone," or "We exceeded the budget"). That stuff happens every day. The question is not, "What happened?" The question is "Why did it happen?" Dig deep, and identify the root cause for these issues. Try to understand and describe why things went wrong. Even successful programs can have flaws and failures along the way. Never say, "We achieved our goals, so nothing went wrong." That just doesn't happen.

❖ **How do we improve**? Learn something. This is the most important part of the retrospective. You need to understand the good and the bad and form an executable plan for maintaining the good and improving the bad.

In 2008, I led the retrospective of the definition of Sandy Bridge, Intel's second-generation CORE™ product line, and this helped me learn and prepare for leading the Skylake definition.

Comparing MNCs and Start-ups

Through my work in start-ups and Intel, I learned to identify and respect the similarities and differences between them. Many of them I've already described.

Perhaps the most important difference lies in the area of responsibilities and authority, which, I remind you, are conjoined twins.

❖ When you work for the big guys, you have a relatively narrow set of responsibilities for a certain domain or function or product or technology or market. This means that you must rely on others to execute their roles properly if the organization is to succeed. Success requires integration and collaboration, sharing of information and resources, and making sure that your work complements the work of others and achieves synergy.

❖ When you work among the little guys, each player typically has a wide set of responsibilities and significant authority. You must often be concerned with and do things beyond your expertise or experience. The smaller crew enables start-ups to be agile, work fast, and adapt in the changing ecosystem.

In both, you develop bridges among individuals, teams, companies, government, industry associations, user groups, nontechnical professionals—the list goes on and on. Those bridges address problems, innovate solutions, and fulfill needs. They are your stepping stones to success.

Chapter 9

൦ଃ଼ଵ

The Military

Leading vs. Commanding

Let's digress a bit to a different area. The business world is very different from the military. Or is it? Although the high-level goals and objectives are quite different—security for the people versus profits for the shareholders—many similarities exist in the strategies and actions you develop and execute. The military is a very hierarchal organization and ranks matter, but in most parts of the military, rank authorizes you to command. It doesn't make you a leader.

People follow officers they respect and look up to them as role models, not just because they have more hardware on their shoulders or more braid on their sleeve. As an officer, you must build a bridge between yourself and

- ❖ the officers and enlisted personnel under your command;
- ❖ fellow officers of equal rank; and
- ❖ the officers who outrank you.

Rank establishes who issues the orders and who assumes the final responsibility for seeing that the job was done properly. Getting the job done right in the military happens in the same way as it does in business or any other organization.

You must show people a bridge between the present and the long-term vision. You have to bridge between what is needed and what is possible. Most importantly, you have to build relationships *with* your people, *among* your people, and *among* your team and other teams.

I entered active duty in the Israeli Navy, part of the Israeli Defense Force (IDF), in March 1990. From day one, I was an officer (a lieutenant), and I was expected to lead people—soldiers, engineers, technicians, even civilians on occasion. I had three periods or roles while on active duty.

Plan A

During my first two years, I served in the navy's electronics workshop of the naval shipyards as a systems engineer. I was responsible for systems engineering and integration of missile boat weapon systems, including missiles—the Harpoon and Gabriel surface-to-surface missiles—and guns—the Phalanx and the 76mm naval gun built by OTO Melara.

I was in my early twenties, and I was expected to command a group of people who were both older than me and much more experienced than I was at what we were doing. Even so, I was in charge. I had both the responsibility and accountability for everything we did. First, I had to establish my place within a group of engineers and technicians, some of which were older than my parents! I also had to direct them in what needed to be done and how it should be done. Some of them were not even military personnel. They were civilians working for the navy.

In none of this did my rank really help me establish my position as their leader. I had to learn as I went, and I had to behave like a leader. I had to earn their respect as a person, as an engineer, and as a member of the military. It was during these days that I first really developed my skill set as a bridge builder between myself and other people. Bridges that would make my work with them effective and would help me drive programs and projects to successful completion.

The Rubber Hit the Road

I remember one incident where I fully realized the importance of my role. I was working on the antenna of the Gabriel surface-to-surface missile (SSM) weapon system, high up on the mast of the ship, together with an older civilian who was a very experienced engineer. Obviously, he had more experience than I had as an engineer, but he was complacent and didn't really care that much about safety protocols. I had to almost force him to wear a safety belt while working in the heights. I remember talking in a very authoritative tone, explaining to him the importance of the safety belt when working aloft. When it was just the two of us up high on the antenna, I had to be the "responsible adult," making sure that both of us were safe while we did our job.

Not a big deal? In fact, it was. As long as he was under my direction, I was responsible for his safety as well as for his work. If I failed to *demand* that proper safety procedures be followed, any accident was, by definition, my fault. A fall from that height could easily have been fatal, and I would've been held responsible even though he was old enough to know better. In many militaries, there's a saying, "It happened on your watch, that makes it your fault."

The Sailor Hit the Sea, and the Sea Hit Back

During these two years, I participated in numerous trial cruises where we'd test and validate the integration and quality of the weapon systems. As the leader, this required me to operate under severe conditions of seasickness and a less-than-stable working surface driven by the waves of the Mediterranean Sea.

More than any time in my life, this is where I learned the importance of perseverance and persistence. Navy people, like many others, are fond of the saying, "When the going gets tough, the tough get going." (To which an old sage added somewhat jokingly, "And the going gets to the not-so-tough and the not-so-tough get not-so-going.") Unfortunately, despite the state of my stomach and others' stomachs, I had to stay the course and keep everybody on track to complete our mission. As military personnel, we know that our enemies (should they attack) are not going to wait for what mariners have long called "fair winds and following seas." They will come at us whenever they feel the situation is most advantageous to them. Even if the sea was rough, and we didn't feel so well (to put it mildly), we had to perform.

Plan B

During the second part of my naval service, I was assigned as chief electronics officer for the transformation of a Sa'ar 4-class into a Sa'ar 4.5-class missile boat.

(*Sa'ar*, by the way, is Hebrew for "storm." They are corvettes—small warships—of, in this case, just under five hundred tonnes and manned by about fifty officers and sailors.)

INS *Romach* was the first time the naval shipyards renovated and upgraded a class 4 to class 4.5 (called the Nirit Model) without the help of the Israeli Shipyards, the original builders of the first Sa'ar 4.5, the INS *Hetz*. As the chief electronics officer of this huge engineering project, I was responsible for installation, integration, and testing of all the electronics systems on the missile boat—weapon systems, navigation systems, electronic warfare systems, command-and-control systems, communication systems, and more. This was a great experience for me, going beyond the borders of my experience in weapon systems. I had to build many new bridges and work with many different types of engineers within the navy and also with civilian engineers working for the different defense systems vendors who were integrating new systems into the missile boat.

These included electrical engineers, mechanical engineers, computer engineers, project managers, and others. I also had to build bridges and work with the combat officers of INS *Romach*, the people who'd be using the systems that we integrated into their newly-rebuilt boat. In many navies, the captain is said to "sit in the center chair." During this project, in some respects, I sat there.

I had to be the bridge—although, for this project, it might be better described as the hub of a wheel with a very large number of spokes—among all the many and very different jobs and people. It was up to me to see that all the participants worked coherently and effectively. My responsibility (my goal) could be summed up as: at the end of the day, the customer—the officers of INS *Romach*—would be satisfied with what they received from the naval shipyard, a new missile boat with new and improved capabilities that enabled them to do a better job protecting the shores and sea-transportation routes of the State of Israel.

That's what we did. We didn't do it because I was a brilliant engineer. We succeeded because I did the work needed to educate myself on what was needed. I kept lines of communication open. I made sure my people and others had what they needed, and we did it all "the navy way."

How did I do that? In most respects, it was just the way I described doing it in my later civilian employment. Moreover, I had the fortune of learning from my friend and mentor Guy Menchik, who is just a bit older than me and served at the same position I held a year earlier in the building of the INS *Hetz*.

Plan C

In my last position at the Israeli Navy, I was stationed at the navy headquarters in Tel Aviv, part of the IDF head-quarters. My role was in the weapon systems world, and I was responsible for leading several projects and programs.

Advanced military organizations work a lot like high-tech. They must always reinvent themselves, developing new solutions to new problems or improved solutions for old problems. If they stay the course, refusing to change, they become as extinct as the dinosaurs, and, potentially, in the same very messy way. It's not enough to be the biggest or the strongest. One has to be the most adaptive to change in order to survive and flourish.

Since the military deals with the physical and cyber worlds, many of the solutions being developed are complex and require high budgets; they involve numerous disciplines and many people and take a long time to define, develop, test, integrate, and deploy. As an engineer, I spent all my time in the navy in the high-tech parts of the navy. By doing, I learned how to operate in a very large high-tech organization, defining and developing highly complex and multidisciplinary systems. Most times they were systems of systems.

The most notable of them all was my role as the first program officer of the Typhoon Naval Stabilized Weapon Station. In business-world terms, I was the first product manager of that system—the first strategic planner, as we would've said at Intel. This was the first time I was involved in the definition of a new system that included many innovations and created a lot of value. I built a bridge between the needs of the Israeli Navy and a multidisciplinary system of systems that delivered a solution for the need.

I worked very closely on the one hand with the customers—the weapon system officers at Israeli Navy Headquarters—and on the other hand, with the developers—several defense contractors such as Rafael Advanced Defense Systems, Israel Aerospace Industries

(IAI), Kollmorgen, Lockheed Martin, and others who were all bidding to be the developers and integrators of the system.

I wrote the request for proposal (RFP), a seminal document that outlined the requirements and specifications of the system, and worked closely with the vendors to help them develop their response to the RFP. When we evaluated the different proposals, we recommended that the navy choose Rafael, as they submitted the proposal most suited to the requirements of the Israeli Navy. This was the first time I led product definition of a highly complex system, acting as a bridge among many different disciplines with conflicting needs and requirements. I learned the importance of developing a relationship with the people you work with—all the stakeholders within your own organization, with the customers, with the suppliers, and with the partners.

This systems integration project was essentially the same work that I later did in systems engineering and strategic planning. You bring people in that are responsible for different types of systems—radar, weapon, navigation, communication, and more—each one built by a different vendor. The development, testing, and installation of each of these subsystems was overseen by its own system (or subsystem) engineer.

That placed me in position to be the systems engineer over all the subsystem engineers and make sure that everything worked together smoothly. This must happen on both personal and technical levels. There are always problems in the integration of parts from multiple vendors. Unfortunately, that leads to a lot of finger-pointing. No one wants to risk his job or his company's contract by admitting they made a mistake. Each side says someone else did something wrong and that's why it's not working. Yet finger pointing is counterproductive, and the systems engineer or product manager or strategic planner needs to bridge between all parties to move forward and resolve the issues.

As the program officer, I became the main connecting point for the technology and the people. When problems arose, I had to mediate. A technical problem became a human problem, and there needed to be a human solution before you could create the technical solution. The goal of that human solution could be described, in general terms, as "these people have to work together in an adult, professional way." That can be tough.

First, I found that it's always important to figure out *the why*, not just *the what*:

❖ Why are we doing this thing the way we're doing it?
❖ Why are we defining this specification like this?

Many times, people get totally focused on what they're doing, what should be done, or what should be defined. It's really important to understand *the why* and to convey it to everybody so they also understand *the why* of what you're doing.

Second, I had to be a really good listener. I needed to be modest enough to accept that I didn't know everything. (In this case, that wasn't particularly hard for me. I was still a twenty-something junior officer dealing with some people who had been doing what they were doing for many, many years.) It was easy for me to go to the experts, ask their advice, and hear their opinions directly from their mouths, and understand their perspectives. Sometimes I had to interview them for hours before I fully understood what they were talking about, because they started using all these terms that to the "uninitiated" might seem like Mandarin or Hindi. Fortunately, when you talk with them enough, read enough, and look at enough examples of comparable systems, you start to understand what they mean. Then I needed to translate this into simple English or Hebrew so the other stakeholders could understand what's going on.

It's a lot of decoding. It's a lot of asking others to have patience because I needed to understand complex subsystems (outside of my then-current experience) sufficiently that I could discuss them intelligently, in simple Hebrew or English, with other experts in completely different domains. I had to become a jack-of-all-trades even though I truly was a master-of-none.

This happened during the definition of the project, during development, during lab testing, during the installation and field testing, and, on occasion, after deployment. Leadership in such situations requires the leader to get past the name-calling and finger-pointing to dig into the systems and identify the real problem, then bring the sides together with a solution that satisfies everyone's needs.

Many times during my military service and long after, this type of situation arose, and it was my responsibility to bring all sides to the table, create an encouraging conversation between them, and devise an effective resolution to the problems. More than anything else, those are the bridges I've seen projects needing.

Looking Back

All these years later, I still feel proud when I hear on the news that the Typhoon system developed by Rafael and deployed on dozens of Israeli Navy fast patrol boats successfully helped protect the state of Israel from terrorists and attackers.

After five years of active duty in the navy, I decided to move to the civilian world. I enjoyed my time in the navy. I learned a lot and developed my skills and experience. However, I decided that I'd never again work for a defense contractor. This was a conscious decision to redirect my efforts to companies that developed and marketed solutions that made the world a better place and improved the quality of life. I consider this decision to be an important part of the bridge to my happiness in life.

I set the uniform aside, but I took some priceless lessons with me:

When you do things like upgrade a warship or define a new weapon system, you have to deal with amazingly complex systems. As the project officer, I had to think about the system and about all the subsystems and make all those things working together efficiently. I had to think about what the system needed to be or do from the perspective of many different stakeholders. So I had to wear many hats:

- ❖ I put on the hat of the users—the officers and crewmembers of the ship that would use this system—to understand with them all their needs and requirements.
- ❖ I also had to put on the hat of the engineers and developers who were creating the subsystems. I had to understand if and how the system could be built and developed in a reasonable time, at a reasonable cost.

❖ I put on the hat of the finance people who were overseeing the financial implications. After all, every project has a budget, and you never have unlimited resources.

Nobody can do this alone. For each and every domain or discipline, you do it together with the people who are experts on that specific domain.

Many times, the language used by those experts is very internal to their own domain. It's their industry jargon or slang. A lot of translation needs to be done, because you cannot go to, let's say the developers and tell them, "I want this system to have a profit margin of eighty-five percent." They wouldn't know what to do with it. You have to help them translate financial dreams into engineering realities.

All this translation and bridging among the different domains will, if you're successful, deliver a holistic system comprising subsystems that cover all aspects, all dimensions, and makes it possible to develop the system within the constraints of the cost, the time, the head count—and doing all of that while fulfilling the needs of the users.

Chapter 10

⊂ଓଅ⊃

Nonprofits

Why Get Involved in Nonprofit Orgs

The capitalist world lacks equity because differences of outcome are a natural consequence of freedom. I'm better at some things than you are, and you're better at other things than I am. That's why we build bridges. That's why we work together. Our skills make up for the lack of skills in others. It's a great system.

But of course, there are downsides. A capitalist society includes people who are less fortunate than others due to their economic background, health conditions, the environment they grew up in, or any of a hundred other factors.

It took me more than twenty years to realize that I needed to pitch in and use my skill set and experience to help bridge the inequities in our society. I had to assume some responsibility and lead some change to help less fortunate people bridge from their harsh situation to a better future, one that would make them happier and help them fulfill their aspirations and potentials.

In early 2014, I decided that I should volunteer in a strategic way to positively impact the lives of others. It was a calling that I felt was deep in my DNA, and perhaps

I inherited it from my grandmother, Hanni Ullmann, who served as general manager of Ahava, a children's and youth village in Kiryat Bialik in the Haifa Bay. (This great lady also established the first Israeli training school for nursery school teachers.) After leading Ahava for almost twenty years, she retired but did not stop working. She founded and volunteered for twenty-five years as the executive director of the Neve Hanna Children's Home. Located in Kiryat Gat, a city in the southern district of Israel, it was the first family-like home for at-risk children and youth in Israel. My grandmother was recognized and highly praised, and she received many awards for her work including the President of the State of Israel Award for Outstanding Volunteering and the President of the Federal Republic of Germany Excellence Award for her life's achievement. She dedicated her life to helping deprived and socially disadvantaged children to overcome their life tragedies and become happy, productive adults. She inspired me to do something similar. However, I didn't want to leave the career in high-tech that I loved, so I had to find a way to bridge between these two worlds.

I also knew that I want the next chapter in my life to be in venture capital—investments in high-tech start-ups. When I analyzed this strategically, I concluded that nonprofit organizations could serve as that bridge between start-ups and venture capital. Seems an odd decision? Let me explain:

Ever since I began my career in start-ups, I always admired the investors. How do they know which start-ups to fund and nourish? In the beginning, it was a mystery to me, like black magic. As I moved along my work in start-ups and Intel, many pieces of the puzzle became clear to me, and I thought I gained a solid grasp of the operational world of start-ups and how they should behave to make them a good fit for big corporations to acquire and integrate.

However, one thing was still missing in my understanding of this world. I did not know how boards of start-ups or corporations worked. I met and talked with board members through the years, but I did not experience it myself. Like my decision that I needed an MBA, I felt this was a missing tool in my skill set.

It's an important piece for someone who wants to become a successful investor, a partner in a venture capital firm. To fill this gap, I decided that I need to get some experience as a member of a board. However, I wanted to "crawl before I walk before I run." This I learned during my days at Intel. It's a strategy that Intel uses frequently in almost everything it does. So I decided that my best approach would be to become a member of the board of a nonprofit association, as a stepping stone toward becoming a board member in a for-profit start-up. This coincided with two other things:

- ❖ First, it's a mature mindset that understood that this was the right time for me to take everything I learned and did in the commercial world and use it to contribute to the society with my time and energy instead of just with my money.
- ❖ Second, a proposal came to my inbox. It was a proposal to join Synergy—a program led by the American Jewish Joint Distribution Committee (also called JDC or "The Joint") that was offered at Intel for senior executives.

This program helped senior executives from the for-profit world to volunteer as board members in the nonprofit world. I was fortunate to meet with the two exceptional ladies who led this program, Ronit Levy-Zilberstein and Osnat Hazan. They helped me understand what kind of nonprofit association is right for me and connected me with Big Brothers Big Sisters of Israel. I then met with Roi Pilpel, their CEO; Esti Shamama, chairwoman of the executive board; and Yossi Freier, another board member and former chairman of their executive board.

When they told me about the history, current activities, and the vision of Big Brothers Big Sisters of Israel, it was love at first sight. I fell in love with the organization and had a strong connection with the important work they were doing. I wanted to be part of it and contribute my experience and expertise. I joined the executive board as a member on April 8, 2014.

Big Brothers Big Sisters of Israel provides long-term mentorship to children and youth who lack a positive parental influence. This Israeli nonprofit organization is one of a few similar organizations internationally in countries like Canada, Australia, and, of course, the well-known Big Brothers Big Sisters of America. The American movement was established in 1904 by Ernest Coulter, a juvenile court clerk who realized that many of the youth coming into court had something in common—they lacked a positive parental influence. For some, a parent or both parents had died, or the dad went to prison and the mom worked day and night to feed them, or some other unfortunate circumstance. This made them more susceptible to risk and easier to become delinquent. He started Big Brothers Big Sisters of America, and it became an important part of American culture, spreading across every state. Today, this organization continues helping at-risk youth, matching them with an adult volunteer who mentors them and acts as a role model.

Big Brothers Big Sisters helps these youths overcome the challenges of life, become happy children and, later, happy adults—productive and participating citizens of their societies. In 2003, Libby Reichman, a social worker, founded Big Brothers Big Sisters of Israel and led the organization for the first eight years, after which she continued to be involved, especially in the Jerusalem area. I had the privilege and honor to volunteer on the executive board of Big Brothers Big Sisters of Israel for many years, and I'm proud to say that during these years, we grew the organization, increasing the positive impact we had on the resiliency of the society in Israel and the lives of thousands of children, youth, and young adults.

The Role of the Executive Board Member

When I started volunteering on the board, I wasn't precisely sure about the role of a board member. Once again, I had to learn on the job.

For those of you who may wonder, that happens all the time in the military, in business, in academia, in government, and in community organizations. On-the-job training (OJT) is alive and well, and we all do it, so don't be afraid of it. I repeat, I specifically joined this board because I lacked certain skills. I traded my experience and my work for what they could teach me. It was a profitable exchange on both sides. That, by the way, is one very good definition of success.

In the beginning, I generally observed what was going on. I looked at and listened to the other board members and consulted with the "Synergy Team," Ronit and Osnat. I learned that the board of a nonprofit is a very important organ of the organization and has several key roles:

- ❖ Develop and lead the vision and strategy of the organization.
- ❖ Hire, manage, and remove the CEO of the organization when necessary.
- ❖ Monitor and ensure corporate governance and regulatory adherence.

In the Israeli system, each and every board member has all of these responsibilities, and all are accountable for them. (Other countries have different rules. You should examine them and understand exactly what you're getting into and agree that you will assume the legal and other responsibilities involved before you sign on.) I came to understand very quickly that these organizations have a tactical/strategic split that must work together closely for the organization to be successful:

- ❖ The tactical leadership is the CEO and the management team. They manage the day-to-day operation of the nonprofit organization. They make the program work.
- ❖ The strategic leadership is the board. They may be called directors or trustees or regents or any number of other titles. Regardless of title, they are the legal stewards of the organization's vision, money,

property, reputation, and all other assets. They define the program.

This was a big change for me. For more than twenty years in the business world, I've led and managed operational groups. I made the program work.

Board members must not interfere with the operational level. They must be involved and committed without intervening. They must not micromanage operations. I came to the realization that a more effective relationship between the board and the management team, especially the CEO, is a partnership type of relationship. Although by stature and long custom, the board is the supervisor and employer of the CEO, it's more effective for them to have a partnership relationship with the CEO, empowering him/her to lead the organization's daily moves. This partner-relationship is symbiotic—both parties need each other and cannot sustain and grow the organization effectively without each other. If they don't collaborate, failure is as certain as anything in the world.

The Role of the Chairman of the Executive Board

The People Are the Power

Under Israel's Nonprofit Associations law, a chairman of the board is not a must-have. Every board member has an equal share of the responsibility and accountability for the organization, as I mentioned. Nevertheless, I learned that the chairman is comparable to the major shareholder or the chairman of a business, whether it's a start-up or larger corporation. I became the chairman of the board of Big Brothers Big Sisters of Israel in

January 2017. At this writing, in 2023, I'm honored and privileged to continue in this capacity. As I grew in my role as chairman, I realized that the chairman has two major functions:

❖ **Leader of the board.** I am responsible for building and maintaining an effective and diversified board comprised of individuals from different disciplines that work coherently together for the benefit of the nonprofit and its beneficiaries.

❖ **Mentor of the CEO.** I am responsible for guiding the CEO in effectively managing the organization and interacting with the board. Sometimes, I think of it as being the big brother of the CEO, being there for him/her in difficult times and acting as a sounding board to help him/her guide the organization.

Throughout the years, I had the honor and privilege of collaborating with excellent board members—all volunteers—who wanted to do good and didn't get a penny for it. Some of them started serving at the board before me, and others were recruited by me and Nati Kashi, who succeeded Roi Pilpel as CEO.

Each of them made an important contribution to the work. They impacted the success of Big Brothers Big Sisters of Israel, and they did all of it because they felt it is important. They wanted to contribute, helping less fortunate youth overcome challenges that were thrust on them, so they could fulfill their potential.

To make our board effective, we always ensured that we had gender equity—half of the board members were women, and half were men. We also ensured we had a diverse and complementary set of skills and experience—finance, accounting, business, education, high-tech, legal, marketing, psychology, welfare, and more. This diversity meant our board had differing opinions and viewpoints, but we combined all of them toward making the best possible decisions and helped the CEO and the management team fulfill the vision of the organization.

The People Are the Purpose

By the way, how do we know we're succeeding? Among other methods, our board members sometimes get out in the field so we can see first-hand if we're getting the job done right.

When you meet the moms of those children and they tell you the story of how their big brothers or big sisters are impacting their children, well, basically, it's not just the children. Our volunteers impact the whole family in a very positive way. Hearing their stories and getting letters from them is very touching and makes you feel good to know that we're doing good for so many families and children.

Sometimes we do roundtables where we bring all the stakeholders of Big Brothers Big Sisters to sit around the same table—parents, volunteers, partners, staff members, and board members. We discuss strategic issues or topics and plans for the organization. We hear those moms and dads. They tell us what impact our programs are having on their family, and it absolutely makes you cry from joy. No joke, no exaggeration.

Replacing the CEO

On December 11, 2017, Roi Pilpel, who'd served as CEO for six and a half years, dropped a bomb. He'd decided to leave to become CEO of another nonprofit organization. I'd been chairman of the board for less than a year, and this came as a big surprise to the board members. Roi told us that he could stay for a couple of months, and afterward, he'd help the new CEO.

We had to act fast. The board decided to hire a recruiting agency that focused on senior positions in nonprofit organizations in Israel to identify candidates and bring them to a CEO recruiting committee that we formed. This became a very intense process. As the clock ticked by, we had to quickly find the best candidate for the job and do his/her onboarding before Roi left our organization for his new position. In fact, we had less than two months for the whole process. We had to quickly build a bridge between Roi and the new CEO, but first, we had to have a new CEO.

With the recruiting agency, we developed a job description and published it in the relevant places. We received 275 resumes and selected the top 23 candidates. The recruiting agency then met with these 23 and provided feedback. From them, we selected 10 candidates to meet with the CEO recruiting committee. The committee selected 3 finalists and assigned them a task: study the ecosystem and Big Brothers Big Sisters of Israel and present to us your vision and a strategy for the organization. These 3 candidates presented their work to the entire executive board, and the new CEO was chosen with a unanimous vote.

On February 12, 2018, two months and one day after Roi gave us his notice, Tomer Tveria and the board signed the agreement that made him the CEO, effective March 1, 2018. We succeeded in our mission to find and recruit a CEO for the organization and ensure continuity and sustainability of the organization. It was a textbook process. We did all the right things and followed the advice and guidelines of experienced experts. Tomer started leading the organization with a lot of help and guidance from Roi, from me, and from the other board members.

Sadly, after less than a year, it became clear that it was not a good match, and on October 16, 2018, Tomer gave us his resignation letter. Both he and the board thought we'd gotten it right. He'd spent ten years as another nonprofit's CEO, and he'd run it well. That's one of the primary reasons we hired him. Unfortunately, our nonprofit operated very differently than that previous organization. Ours required a slightly different skill set. Had he been able to stay with us a few years, he'd have acquired those skills and been great, but we didn't have the time or resources to train him, so we parted on good terms, and we went back to square one.

Once again, we had to find and recruit a new CEO for the organization but this time, we had to act even quicker. We were in a turbulent condition, as the financial situation of the organization was dire, and the employees were under a lot of stress. Big Brothers Big Sisters of Israel was at real risk of shutting down. The executive board stepped up and saved the organization. Though this isn't a normal expectation of board members, we kept the organization going with personal loans and a hands-on approach, helping the team leads—Dorit Weshler, Shlomit Loya, and Daniel Aviram—continue running the operations, providing service to our hundreds of volunteers as well as the hundreds of youths we served and supported. At the same time, we embarked on a new CEO search.

For this hunt, we chose to forego the help of a recruiting agency, primarily because we didn't have the money to spend on one. It was a freestyle process, but we could leverage some of the work we'd done in the previous year's process. On November 8, 2018, less than one month after Tomer's notice, we signed an agreement with Nati Kashi to become the CEO, effective November 20, 2018. This time, we succeeded beyond our wildest dreams. Nati has been leading the organization through the rebound period of 2019, recovering from the difficult 2018, passing through the difficult COVID-19 period of 2020–21, into the growth period of 2022–23, and, hopefully, for many more years. Nati is the perfect leader for Big Brothers Big Sisters of Israel—the right person at the right time and the right place. He brought with him a wealth of experience and expertise in both the business and social welfare domains. I greatly enjoy partnering with Nati, as we grow the organization and expand to new areas such as youth-at-risk in boarding schools, leadership programs for high school students, helping young kids improve their reading and writing skills, helping children with disabilities, and much more.

Incentivizing the CEO

A nonprofit board has an important role in helping to ensure continuity, sustainability, and organizational growth, and must incentivize the CEO toward those objectives. To that end, when I became chairman, I decided to leverage the best-known methods (BKM) of business organizations and conduct an annual performance review of the CEO, focusing on three main aspects, as described in Chapter 8:

❖ Accomplishments
❖ Strengths
❖ Development

Starting in 2021, we enhanced our methodology with the CEO Performance Model that was developed in December 2020 by a board member, the late Ofer Kam. Ofer was a dear friend and a significant contributor and member of the board for many years until his death from cancer in January 2022. The performance model we created and refined each year was driven from the strategic plan we developed for the organization. It includes the key objectives and goals that we, as an organization, and the CEO, as an individual, need to achieve in leading the organization and fulfilling our vision. It's important to include several key objectives, some of which are quantifiable, and some of which are more qualitative in nature. For each, we developed a scale of three to five options to enable grading of the CEO performance along each of the specific metrics defined. The performance model was developed together with the CEO to ensure that he and the board were aligned with the expected performance.

Comparison of For-Profit vs. Nonprofit Organizations

Nonprofit organizations are very different from for-profit organizations, right?

It can be said that the high-level goals and objectives are very different: In nonprofit organizations, you focus on solving problems in society that are not solved by the government or business. In for-profit organizations, you focus on increasing returns for the shareholders. However, in many respects, successful nonprofits and for-profits follow the same recipe. It bears repeating:

All organizations are ultimately "for-profit" organizations.

The designations refer only to money taken in but not spent and where that money goes. In what the law calls a "for-profit," that money goes to organization's stockholders-owners. In what the law calls a "nonprofit," that money goes to further realize the organization's vision, delivering greater value to society.

However, both types of organizations must define a "profit" and consistently earn a profit, or they cease to exist. In Big Brothers Big Sisters of Israel, our "profit" was youth who ceased to be at-risk and became happy, responsible, successful adults. You can't demonstrate that as easily as a business demonstrates it with a profit-and-loss statement, but if a nonprofit isn't successful at demonstrating it, potential donors don't donate. It's very much like a start-up courting angels and VCs for investments. You must show them that you create value and capture value ("profit").

What Works There Works Here

In fact, many strategies and actions you need to develop and execute to achieve success are essentially the same in both types of organizations.

In both, you must build many bridges between what is needed and what is possible; between what you'd like to do and what you can do; between the present and the future; between different disciplines; and of course, among a wide variety of people.

The same BKMs that work in the commercial world work in the noncommercial world:

❖ You must develop your organization's vision and mission, along with your short-, medium-, and long-range strategy—typically for one year, three years, and five years, respectively, but sometimes for much longer.

❖ You must hire the right people and create the optimized organizational structure to support and implement the strategies.

❖ You must motivate and incentivize the participants (employees, volunteers, donors and beneficiaries) at all levels.

❖ You must listen to the participants and understand their needs and aspirations.

❖ You must form partnerships with other organizations to bridge the gaps between what you would like to do and what you cannot do on your own.

❖ You must develop metrics and KPIs (key product indicators); measure and monitor them all the time; and strive to improve and adapt to the changing environment.

In the final analysis, the practices of effective leadership are universal. They always require adaptation to each individual situation, but they always work.

A Case Study

Since we're talking about all the meaningful bridges, something recently happened that presents a perfect example of long-term bridge-building. I mentioned earlier that people do business with people with whom they feel comfortable because they have done business previously or have some other preexisting connection.

Not long ago, I went to Deloitte, one of the Big 4 accounting and consulting companies—along with Ernst & Young (EY), KPMG, and PricewaterhouseCoopers (PwC). Deloitte's Israel offices are on the thirty-seventh floor of the Azrieli Center Towers in Tel Aviv, a prime piece of office real estate.

I went as chairman of the board of Big Brothers Big Sisters of Israel because Deloitte was kind enough to contribute a four-hour workshop where we developed marketing strategy, the website, and things like that.

One of the Deloitte people leading the workshop was a lady whose last name I recognized. I asked her, "Are you related to [this fellow] that has the same last name that I know from NYU?"

That fellow was a Stern School of Business alumnus, like myself, whom I'd met maybe twenty years earlier through the alumni club. In fact, he and I (and others) were, at that time, in discussions as part of what I'm doing at NextLeap Ventures, with the potential of creating a business relationship with him on a project.

This young lady from Deloitte was, in fact, his daughter. Of course, we immediately pulled out the smartphone, took a selfie together, and sent it to her dad, my fellow alumnus and potential business partner. We may have passed a total population of eight billion on planet earth, but at times, it is still a small world.

Bridges should be built to last a thousand years to be used by successive generations.

Bringing Nonprofits and For-Profits Together

Here's one more point before we leave the nonprofit world:

There's an organization in Israel called *Tmura*[15] that operates as a public VC. When a high-tech start-up does a round of financing/investment, they can allocate options in the company to Tmura for no charge, as a donation. These options—equity in the start-up—are held by Tmura. When the start-up has an exit, let's say, it gets acquired by another company, the options acquire real value. The start-up can then guide Tmura, telling them, "The money you're now getting from us due to the exit will go to these nonprofit organizations."

That's exactly what happened with the first exit at NextLeap Ventures. The start-up was Nanofabrica, which does 3D printing at a one-micron resolution.[16] We led an equity financing round together with M12—Microsoft Venture Capital, the corporate venture capital group of Microsoft Inc. About eighteen months after we led the round, Nanofabrica was acquired by Nano Dimension. When we did the equity round in Nanofabrica, we allocated options to Tmura, and when we completed the exit, Tmura received a fair amount of money from the

---

[15] "Tmura" is the Hebrew word for change or metamorphosis and means value for money; it is also a play on the word "truma", which means donation.
[16] "1 micron" is "1 micrometer" or 1/1,000,000th (1×10^{-6}) of a meter. 1 inch = 25,400 microns.

buyer. Since Nanofabrica donated the options to Tmura, we (the company and the investors) chose the recipients of that money. Some of it went to Big Brothers Big Sisters of Israel.

Of course, NextLeap Ventures isn't the only company doing this. A lot of companies do it, and because of their generosity, many millions of dollars have been donated.

Chapter 11

C33∑⊃

Venture Capital

Bootstrapping a Venture Capital Firm

A New World

Having chronicled my journey through my time in the military, start-up, and multinational-corporation worlds, we finally come to the investor world.

Venture capital firms are the bridge between money and innovation. They invest money in start-ups and foster innovations that create and capture value. That was our goal when we organized NextLeap Ventures. It was an investment firm, but it was also a start-up, so we had to bootstrap this firm into existence.

I'd now spent eleven years in start-ups and another eleven in a major international corporation, and so I spoke fluently the languages of both. When I decided to leave Intel, I went intentionally into the high-tech investment world. My goal was simple:

❖ Become a partner in a venture capital firm.
❖ Invest in early stage start-ups.
❖ Help them succeed in changing the world.

❖ Earn money for myself and the other investors who would join me.

Both my parents worked to change the world, or at least a small corner of it, by making the lives of individuals better. I wanted to build on their legacy and tackle the bigger problems of humanity, solve them, and leave a legacy of my own, a positive impact on the world. I adopted an ancient African proverb as my motto, in many things I do in life:

"If you want to go fast, go alone; if you want to go far, go together."

With this decision firmly in mind, I looked at the few options for how to become a player—not to brag, because that's not the point, but I wanted to be an important, leading, and meaningful player in the venture capital ecosystem. Very quickly, I realized that it wouldn't be possible for me to join an existing VC as a partner because I didn't have experience in VCs. Why would anybody agree to take me as a partner?

I considered going into the VC arena by stepping back a few paces, starting as an associate, principle, or something like that. I'd then start to climb the ladder within the hierarchy of a VC owned and managed by others. At this point in my life, this didn't feel like the right option for me.

So I asked myself, what was I left with? The answer was obvious: I would start a new VC.

Naturally, because I have a great belief in communities and in doing things together, I said, "I'm not going to do this alone. If I do this alone, I will fail." I knew I needed partners, and I started looking at my options for that plan. About this time, I heard of a group called AfterDox.

Amdocs is a very big telecom charging and billing company—big in Israel, big worldwide. It takes care of a lot of the charging and billing in many telecom and cellular networks across the globe. AfterDox is an Amdocs alumni investment group, comprised of former Amdocs employees who joined forces to invest in start-ups. This is where I got the initial idea on how to create NextLeap Ventures.

We (me and my NextLeap Ventures partners) met several times with the AfterDox people in order to learn from them. Ultimately, we developed a very different approach on how we do things. We're now proud to say those meetings, combined with our own expertise and experience, allowed us to develop our own strategy and prove to ourselves and the world that it is successful.

Speaking of partners, I called four friends and colleagues with whom I've worked in the Intel Strategic Planning and Business Development Group—Yoav Hochberg, Ronny Korner, Ido Lapidot, and Yosi Govezensky. They left Intel in 2015 and 2016, and I left in September 2017. I asked them to join me in building a bridge from my dream to our future. In October 2017, we founded NextLeap Ventures as the investment group of former Intel employees and, after a short while, expanded it to an investment group for former and current Intel employees.

This is actually a nice story. When we started, we thought, "We'll have only former Intel employees." Well, as it turned out, many of our friends who still worked at Intel told us, "Why are you excluding us? You're former Intel employees, and we're future former Intel employees, right? Everybody will leave Intel at some point in time." We couldn't argue with logic like that.

Also, we started with Israelis only, and here again, when our friends in the USA heard about what we were doing, they convinced us to expand to include Americans as well. That's exactly what we did a year and a half after we started.

We developed a methodology that we felt would increase the probability of success for the start-ups and, therefore, increase the return on investment for our investors. However, since we all started our professional careers as engineers, we didn't feel it would be wise or ethical to go and get other people's money before we had a working prototype—a proof-of-concept, if you will—which clearly demonstrated that our methodology worked.

A New Way of Investing

We started with what we called "Fund I." It was a combination of a VC, an angels club, and crowdfunding. Unlike typical VCs, we work in cycles. At the time I wrote this book (2023), we'd already completed eight cycles. Our first three cycles were led by the five partners of NextLeap Ventures and allowed Israeli investors only. In February 2019, we added three more partners in Silicon Valley—Dan Cohen, Rami Caspi, and Richard Schank. We'd known Dan and Rami for many years—they were both former Intel employees—and Richard was a good friend and colleague of Rami for many years. At that time, we opened "Fund I" for American investors in addition to our Israeli investors.

Here's a note about the partners of NextLeap Ventures. Among the eight partners, we have more than two hundred years of experience in almost every aspect of high-tech—strategy, business development, sales, marketing, technology (semiconductor, systems engineering, hardware, software, etc.), product, intellectual property, manufacturing, operations, finance, and more. It's what one would call a dream team.

We built a bridge to success in the form of a well-thought methodology that works in cycles. We conduct one or two cycles per year. A cycle starts with us—all partners of NextLeap Ventures—looking at somewhere in the neighborhood of one thousand start-ups, all of which are located in Israel, where we focus. As there are more than seven thousand start-ups in Israel at any given time, there's an abundance of opportunities. So you might think it's very simple to choose where to invest, right?

In fact, it can be very, very difficult. A thorough selection process requires considerable expertise and sufficient time to do "due diligence" in identifying those start-ups that are ahead of the pack, those opportunities that have the highest potential to succeed in creating value, delivering value, and capturing value. By this, I mean reaching an exit point where the investors "meet the money" and get serious returns on their investments.

How did NextLeap Ventures determine those exceptional start-ups? First, we used networking. Among the partners, we have access to a community of around thirty thousand high-tech people in Israel. Most of these contacts are one or two degrees of separation from the partners. Intel is the largest private employer in Israel with somewhere around fifteen thousand employees. About seven thousand of these work in the company's R&D centers, some five thousand work in manufacturing, and the remaining three thousand or so work at the company's affiliates—companies acquired by Intel but left to operate, to a large degree, independently, including Mobileye, Habana Labs, and Moovit. The company has three R&D centers based in Haifa, Petah Tikva, and Jerusalem, as well as a semiconductor manufacturing facility in Kiryat Gat.

In addition, Israel is home to well over fifteen thousand people working in its high-tech sector who used to work for Intel. Here are some distinguished alumni:

- ❖ Eyal Waldman left to start Mellanox, then sold it to nVidia for $7 billion in 2020.
- ❖ Rony Friedman left to become the vice president in charge of Apple Israel's R&D center.
- ❖ Uri Frank left to become the vice president in charge of Google Semiconductor's R&D center in Israel.
- ❖ Raviv Melamed left to found and serve as CEO of Vayyar Imaging, which became a unicorn in June 2022.
- ❖ Mooly Eden retired and became the chairman of the executive committee of the University of Haifa.
- ❖ Dadi Perlmutter retired and became the chairman of the board of the Israel Innovation Institute as well as chairman of the board and director in several start-ups.

A brief side note here: One out of ten Israelis who have founded *unicorns*—private companies with a net worth of more than $1 billion—previously drew paychecks as Intel executives. Intel Israel is a great place to learn the business of innovation.

This core community of thirty thousand people provides us with access to the most innovative start-ups in Israel, some of them founded by former Intel executives. We evaluate about a thousand of them in each cycle, and after a few months, we choose the top sixty. We then roll through a second round of analysis, selecting the top thirty. An even deeper, third round of analysis yields a list of the top twenty start-ups. The fourth round cuts the list to fifteen, followed by a fifth round trimming that number to ten. The sixth round reduces the candidate roll to just seven. The seventh and final round sees us deciding on the top five out of that initial one thousand—just one-half of one percent of the original list.

Those last-five-standing start-ups are investment-worthy. That is to say, all the partners of NextLeap Ventures—the investment committee—believe that we should invest in each of these. A typical VC firm would then go and invest in all five of them, but we are *not* a typical VC firm. There's one more hurdle for the start-ups to overcome.

The founders of the last-five-standing start-ups get invited to a "pitch event." The audience is about a hundred current and former Intel executives from all disciplines:

- ❖ Investment professionals who are working or previously worked for Intel Capital, Intel's highly reputed in-house venture capital unit, founded in 1991
- ❖ Research and development executives from both the hardware and software domains

❖ Manufacturing professionals from the Intel Kiryat Gat fab, including scientists and operation experts
❖ Business and marketing executives responsible for global business success
❖ Finance people, IT, HR, operations, security, lawyers, accountants, and more

Every aspect of a successful business is represented in this audience.

Prior to the pitch event, we hold extensive dry run sessions with the presenting start-ups. We help them prepare for the pitch event. We bring them to a simulated pitch event, where they present their ten-minute pitch to all partners of NextLeap Ventures, and then we spend more than an hour giving them explicit feedback that helps them fine tune their story, pitch, body language, and many more things so they are fully prepared for a successful pitch at the actual pitch event. At the end of the dry run (sometimes there's more than one dry run for a start-up as they rehearse and refine their pitch), I usually tell each and every start-up, "We are really excited you are one of the five start-ups presenting at our pitch event, and we really hope that you will win and get selected as one of the top three. Bear in mind, that I tell this to the other four start-ups as well." And then I smile. Smiling is always good practice in situations like that, and actually in most situations.

At the pitch event, each start-up presents a ten-minute pitch to the audience, after which, the voting starts. Each member of the audience ranks the five start-ups, from one to five. While the system is open for voting, the start-ups host the audience in their booth just as they would host potential customers at a trade show. The audience members can ask the founders any questions where they need clarification or expansion and get a demo or a glimpse of their prototypes. They also talk among themselves and exchange views and opinions. This is called deliberation, and it has been shown in academic research to help individuals and teams reach better decisions.

The voting ends after about thirty minutes. The audience goes back to the auditorium to listen to a keynote speech by a notable industry figure. Among the keynote speakers we've hosted over the years are Andrew Abir, Orna Berry, Eli Groner, Meirav Harnoy, Yanki Margalit, Dadi Perlmutter, Yonit Golub Serkin, and Eyal Waldman. Some of those names you've read before in this book. They are all among the top echelon of Israel's high-tech industry.

After the keynote ends, the results are announced, and three winning start-ups come to the stage to receive their certificate. We call this methodology the "Wisdom of the INTELligent Crowd." Following the pitch event, we enter full due diligence and deal negotiation with the three winning start-ups, and typically, we end up investing in all three.

Our first three investments occurred in June 2018, the result of our first pitch event in December 2017. Since then, we've successfully completed eight cycles, and at the time of writing this book, we are in the middle of our ninth cycle. These first eight cycles resulted in our investing in a total of twenty-three companies over the course of five years. Throughout this process, we build a bridge between the start-up and potential investors who would join a special purpose vehicle (SPV) we establish for investment in the start-up. The SPV is a limited partnership that invests in a single company. Each SPV is separate from any other.

Our investors join each SPV as limited partners, so they must be convinced they're investing in the right company. To that end, we do *deep dives*. These are ninety-minute meetings between start-up founders and the potential investors who've expressed their willingness to look into that start-up. During the deep dives, the potential investors get to know the CEO and other founders and learn more about their venture—vision, business, market, technology, product, team, traction, financials, and more.

In many deep dives, it becomes apparent that some of the potential investors can help the start-up with introductions to potential customers or partners or with solving technology or business challenges. In one of the deep dives, someone asked the CEO, "Given the relatively small amount of money you expect to get from us, why did you 'waste your time' preparing and presenting in the pitch event, then the deep dive, and so on?"

The CEO gave an honest and very clever response. He pointed his hand at those sitting around the table and said, "You see all this brain power? I want *you* to invest in us because that means you'll be using all this brain power to help us succeed. You'll have a vested interest in our success, so you'll naturally help create that success. As a start-up, we need all the help we can get." It was the best answer you can expect from a CEO—a direct and intelligent answer to a direct and valid question by a potential investor.

The Money

For our "Fund I," where we raised more than $20 million, we had four sources of funding:

❖ All the partners of NextLeap Ventures invested in all our start-ups from our own personal funds. As the saying goes, "We put our money where our mouth is." We do this because we truly believe that investing money in our investment framework has a relatively high probability of success and can provide a relatively high return-on-investment.

❖ Our Intel friends and colleagues—current and former Intel executives in Israel and the USA. Some of them join all our investments while some join only a subset. Which investment SPV they join is entirely up to them.

❖ High-net-worth individuals (HNWIs) often join our investments. Again, some join all and some join select SVPs. These HNWIs come to us directly or through partnerships we have with several family offices, such as Rosetta Investments, led by Orit Raviv Swery, or Olympus Financial Strategy, led by Yair Sapir.

❖ Partnerships formed with foreign companies, such as DiveDigital in Germany, led by Gil Bachrach, Christopher Gersten, and Roland Vollath; or Kyto Technology & Life Science in the USA, led by Paul Russo. Both companies are experienced investors with networks in their respective business worlds that are both deep and wide. Each of them joined several of our investments, and we consider our partnerships with them to be an excellent long-term relationship that brings a lot of value to all parties involved—to them, to us, and to the start-ups we jointly invest in.

The bridges we've built with our investors and partners are what make us successful, and we maintain those bridges meticulously. As I said earlier in this book, no wood, steel, or stone bridge just sits there; it is subject to wind, rain, snow, sun, traffic, earthquakes—the list of stresses goes on and on. Without proper inspections and maintenance, that bridge will never stand as long as it should.

We like the people we deal with. We respect them and enjoy working with them. We know that they trust us, and we make sure never to endanger their trust. We have to be transparent. All the facts and figures are open to inspection in every investment we undertake, and we're attentive to their needs and concerns. Our goal remains "to exceed expectations; to do the right thing, at the right time, in the right way."

We've followed this structure for every one of our "Fund I" portfolio companies, and we're satisfied that it represents the best system for what we hoped to accomplish. And indeed, success can already be seen. After investing in twenty-three companies, we already had two exits—two of our portfolio companies were acquired by a larger company, and we were able to distribute the proceeds from the sale to our investors and ourselves. We had a nice "multiple" on our investment, so we are all happy. (If you invested $1 million in a start-up and received $5 million at the exit, that's a multiple of five). The rest of the companies—all twenty-one of them—are still up and running, making good progress as they increase their valuations, revenue, head count, and impact on the world. This by itself is far superior to how well start-ups statistically perform. Overall, more than 90 percent of start-ups fail and shut down.

NextLeap Ventures—The Next Generation

Following the success of our "Fund I," we created our Fund II, which operates on a different basic premise: Fund II operates as a limited partnership that invests in fifteen to twenty start-ups, giving the investors a good diversification across industries and risk profiles. These investors join one limited partnership as limited partners, so they must be convinced they're investing in the right team, specifically, the right general partner (that's NextLeap Ventures), which selects and manages the investments. Other than that, the methodology for selecting start-ups for investments continues to be the cycles and pitch events methodology of "Fund I," for most of the investments that Fund II makes. Since this methodology can sometimes be too slow, we've decided that a small portion of our investments will be made quicker by the investment committee, allowing us to participate in some investment opportunities that are too good to miss out.

Helping Your Start-ups Succeed

As part of our investment in start-ups, we provide them with our virtual accelerator. We typically get a seat on their board, sometimes as a member with voting power and sometimes merely as an observer. One of the NextLeap Ventures partners is assigned as our point person for the start-up and meets regularly with the CEO. We provide them with mentorship as well as connect them with other investors, partners, customers, and potential hires. We help them develop their strategy, their business, their organization. We act as their sounding board, as they consider new and improved ways of addressing the many challenges they face—the "growing pains" common to new businesses—while increasing their valuation, revenue, and profits.

As one of the NextLeap Ventures' co-founders and managing partners, I participate in the boards of five start-ups, again, on some as a member and on others as an observer. At the time of writing of this book, I work closely with Dr. Ziv Yekutieli of Mon4t, Yossi Abu of TechsoMed, Shani Toledano of HT BioImaging, Zeev Efrat and Oshri Cohen of Cybord, and Eyal Zor of Airwayz. Each of these start-ups was and is led by an exceptional individual, and they are all disrupting the markets they operate in, delivering solutions to big problems that are affecting humanity around the world.

My partnership with them has been a relationship with mutual benefits. I learned a lot from them, and I think they learned something from me. Together, we collaborated to ensure that their start-up created and captured value and that everything pointed to the desired eventual exit from the company of our investment group. That exit can come in a variety of ways that enable the investors to "meet the money," which is to say, get the return on their investment. It can be an acquisition. We've already had two such exits: Concertio was acquired by Synopsis (where Yoav Hochberg was our point person), and Nanofabrica was acquired by Nano Dimension (where Ido Lapidot was our point person). It can also be an IPO in the public stock exchange or a significant growth of profits that enable distributing dividends to the shareholders.

I've found that participating in boards of for-profit and nonprofit organizations is very similar. In both cases, you have to guide the ship, helping the captain (that is, the CEO) steer the proper course, being careful not to overpower the CEO or micromanage the organization. It's vital to empower the CEO and make him/her feel that you trust them and are convinced they're the right person at the right time to lead the organization to success and the fulfilment of its vision. You have to be consultative and not authoritative in the way you behave as this will make the bridge you've built stronger and longer.

As a board member or observer, you partner with the CEO. You help him/her and you help the start-up do the best it can to deliver value to the shareholders and investors.

The Value of Networking

In my thirty-year career, I've learned to appreciate the value of networking above all other assets.

Networking is a fundamental concept that underlies everything we do at NextLeap Ventures to create and capture value. Humans are social animals. Scientists have shown that interactions with other humans improve our mental health. Social interactions are equally important in business. We need other people for almost everything we do in the business world. The pay-it-forward strategy works every time: Give before you get. Help people now, and you ensure that they will help you later.

Networking enables teamwork. We get things done more effectively in a group that's more than coworkers or colleagues. They're friends. This is true in business, sports, nonprofit organizations, and every other aspect of life. Working together helps us solve big problems that require diverse expertise.

I repeat the African proverb and the Belgian draft horse analogy:

"If you want to go fast, go alone; if you want to go far, go together."

"A single Belgian can pull a load of eight thousand pounds while two can pull three times as much."

It is all about, in a single word: *synergy*.

When we work (or play or study) with people, we develop mutual trust and respect. The longer and more intensely we work (or play or study) together, the more productive the relationship becomes, allowing us to leverage each other's expertise, experience, and networks.

We all have many networks, and it's important to nurture them, continuously increasing their size and quality, when seeking long-term success. Some networks that I cherish and nurture to this day include the following:

School

From kindergarten through high school, we spend a lot of time with people about the same age as us. We're still young, and the relationships we developed with them are still strong, having lasted for many decades now. When you run into a friend from your childhood, you connect with them quickly because of the shared or similar experiences in your memories. You can joke about the same teachers and remember the parties you enjoyed together.

Youth Groups

During your adolescence, movements such as the scouts or religious groups, such as BBYO, play a big role as you grow and become an adult. It's an excellent framework to meet friends who you may not know from school or your neighborhood. You do things together, go to camps and field trips, and volunteer and absorb the values that form your character for life.

Military Service

In Israel, military service begins at age eighteen. Three years are required for men and two for women. Ask any veteran—wearing the same uniform creates strong bonds between people that can come into play later in life, often in start-ups, large corporations, or investment firms. In the Israel Defense Forces, you spend significant time with peers from different educational and socioeconomic backgrounds. You go through hardships together, living in a small room (or tent), sleeping in bunk beds, and using public showers. You might even go into battle together, where you need to trust and protect each other. Many of the start-ups in Israel have co-founders who met in the army, navy, or air force, and many VCs have partners who met each other there as well. Some specific units have strong alumni networks, where people who served in the same place help each other, fostering business relationships, and advancing their careers. For example, I'm a member of a large WhatsApp group for all alumni of my navy unit, and we frequently share ideas and relationships that help us in the business world. While these relationships differ in countries without compulsory military service, I believe it's one reason for Israel's success in high-tech innovation.

University

I have found tremendous value by participating in the NYU Alumni Club. In fact, several of my company's business partners originally connected with me through the club's chapter in Israel, which I co-founded and where I've been proud to volunteer as president since 2014. I maintain close relationships with many NYU alumni in Israel by participating in all our club events and frequently communicating with my fellow alumni. For example, when I co-founded NextLeap Ventures, I reached out to Orit Raviv Swery and started collaborating with her, as described in Chapter 2.

Business

At Intel, I learned a very important lesson: When a conflict emerges during a business project and you must choose between meeting the project goals or maintaining good relationships with people, you always choose the relationships. Projects end, but relationships continue to be important afterwards. Nurture your network with people from the companies where you've worked. Look into business alumni networks like Intel Alumni. I worked for Intel for eleven years before leaving to found NextLeap Ventures. We now leverage the community of current and former Intel employees by inviting them to our pitch events. This wisdom-of-the-intelligent-crowd approach helps us utilize the diversified backgrounds of people we trust and respect—trust and respect which they (and we) earned while working together or while working with mutual acquaintances.

Volunteering

When you volunteer, you come to know other volunteers who have pledged their time and energy for a cause you believe in. I consider myself very fortunate to have been part of the board of Big Brothers Big Sisters of Israel and serve as chairman of the executive board. Beyond the help we provide to at-risk youth, it's also been an opportunity for me to make new friends and form new business relationships. I highly recommend that everyone who can should find an organization where you can do strategic volunteering. Some might say that volunteering is strictly a giving proposition. I disagree wholeheartedly. To ensure your volunteering remains a positive part of your life story for the long-term, it needs to be a mutually-beneficial relationship. You must give and get. In my view, the best volunteer situation meets three main criteria:

- ❖ It helps address a gap or a need in society on a large scale.
- ❖ It enables you to utilize your expertise while learning new skills and garnering further experience.
- ❖ It generates relationships with others who can help you in your business world.

Sports

Whether you play team sports or just work out in the gym, it's always more fun doing it with friends. When you sweat together, you talk, share achievements, and create memories that strengthen your relationship. Many times, people collaborate with their sports buddies and, many times, work colleagues play together.

Music

Although I don't play any instrument, I have often observed that playing music together fosters close relationships between people. Similar to sports, these relationships can be leveraged for the business world as well.

Friends

Your friends are the people you like the most. You choose to spend time with each other for no better reason than you enjoy each other's company. You like being around them, enjoy doing fun things with them, and you want to spend more time together. Friends can become business partners, and business partners can become friends.

Family

Your family is the most important network you have, as it is unconditional and lifelong. You spend your holidays with them. You celebrate life events with them, from weddings, through births of babies, to funerals of grandparents, aunts and uncles, and, eventually, siblings and cousins. Maintaining a solid, loving relationship with family is the best guarantee that your life will be happy.

Networking is all about relationships—about building bridges with and among people. Relationships make us more productive and effective, enable us to reach higher goals, and make us happy. If you take nothing else away from this book, take this advice:

Proactively grow networks in all the different areas of your life, and proactively work to maintain strong ties within those networks.

This might be the single most important factor that will help you fulfill your aspirations and enjoy life.

Why Invest in Start-ups?

Diversification is key to a healthy financial portfolio that maximizes returns for investors. A typical portfolio would include public market stocks, bonds, and real estate, plus an amount of cash available for emergencies. Start-up (private growth companies) investments are a great spice to add to your financial portfolio. Research shows that private markets outperform public markets throughout the business cycle, and internal rates of return (IRR) pick up following recessions. This is due to many reasons, and here are the major ones:

❖ **Lower valuations enable better multiples**. When you invest in early-stage start-ups, their valuations are low, and if you have the patience to hold your shares until the start-up exits (that is, M&A or IPO), there is a potential for a very high multiple.
❖ **Lower impact of government policies and regulations**. Public companies are subject to many policies and regulations (such as SEC quarterly and annual reports) that often slow their progress and, therefore, limit their ability to bring higher returns for investors.
❖ **Faster response to crisis**. Start-ups, because they're smaller organizations, are more agile. Large, long-established corporations have more inertia. They have policies, politics, traditional ways of doing things, and bureaucracies—all of which slow their response time to quickly-evolving market conditions.

Smaller organizations, with fewer decision-makers and less internal red tape, can respond quickly to changing market conditions, pivot their business if needed, and move forward in a zigzag path towards producing significant value growth.

❖ **Low correlation with public markets**. Early-stage private companies generally have a low correlation with traditional asset classes, such as stocks and bonds.

The best investors allocate more than 10 percent of their portfolio to private equity, and most of them have more than 5 percent of their portfolio in start-ups or VCs. For example, university endowment funds, which are some of the best investors in the market, invest even more in private equity (PE). According to a report by Moonfare, the US average endowment allocation to PE during the decade 2009 through 2018 was 15 percent, providing an annualized return of 8.5 percent, while the most successful fund—the Yale Endowment—allocated 33 percent of their portfolio to PE, generating an 11 percent annualized return over the course of these ten years.[17]

On the other hand, of course, investing in start-ups has two major drawbacks: They entail considerably more risk than larger, established companies with secure market share, and they provide limited liquidity. It's risky because of the high volatility—that is, most start-ups fail, as high as 20 percent in their first year, 50 percent within

[17] Moonfare Germany, "Private Equity in a Portfolio Perspective the Last Free Lunch?," n.d., https://assets-global.website-files.com/5ffb7 d86352880856dbd363e/60f67d5a9b4820871de727f5_60001 0b065a10f197a44a538_Private-Equity-in-a-Portfolio-Perspective. pdf.

five years, and 65 percent within ten years, according to some surveys.[18,19] Only a handful succeed long enough to provide a ROI. Research also shows that it takes more than ten years on average for a start-up to do an exit and return money to their investors.

Finally, the X factor of investing in start-ups is impact. Successful start-ups typically disrupt markets and solve really big problems facing humanity (such as affordable global communications) in a more efficient manner than large corporations or governments ever have. If you want to impact our world in a positive way, you should consider investing in start-ups that address the big problems of the world. You'll have a chance to help create a meaningful impact, and you'll feel like you're really putting your money to good use.

The NextLeap Ventures "Fund I" diversified portfolio of companies includes start-ups that address some of the important areas of our world. At the time of writing this book, these included the following:

❖ **Mobility**—GuardKnox, Carrar, Airwayz, Marine Edge, and SonicEdge
❖ **Healthcare**—Mon4t, Magentiq Eye, TechsoMed, HT BioImaging, Sanolla, and Geneyx
❖ **Computing and communication**—Concertio (exited), ZutaCore, flexiWAN, and New Photonics
❖ **Software and data**—Dataloop, Shield-IoT, and Kaholo

---

[18] Josh Howarth, "Start-up Failure Rate Statistics," Exploding Topics (Exploding Topics, March 16, 2023), https://explodingtopics.com/blog/start-up-failure-stats.

[19] Sean Bryant, "How Many Start-ups Fail and Why?," Investopedia (Dotdash Meredith, November 26, 2022), https://www.investopedia.com/articles/personal-finance/040915/how-many-start-ups-fail-and-why.asp.

❖ **Industry 4.0**—Nanofabrica (exited), Polymertal, Wadis, Cybord, and Enzymit

Some of them are addressing cybersecurity threats—GuardKnox, flexiWAN, and Shield-IoT.

Several of them are addressing sustainability and climate change—Carrar, Airwayz, Marine Edge, ZutaCore, New Photonics, Polymertal, Wadis, and Enzymit.

Most of them are using AI to deliver value in their respective domains—Airwayz, Marine Edge, Mon4t, Magentiq Eye, TechsoMed, HT BioImaging, Sanolla, Geneyx, Concertio, Dataloop, Shield-IoT, Cybord, and Enzymit.

The Start-up to Choose for Investment

After half a decade working with my partners at NextLeap Ventures and having seen thousands of companies seeking investors for early stage, high-tech start-ups, I think we've developed a pretty good sense for what makes a first-rate candidate for start-up investment.

Notice that I say "a first-rate candidate"; I don't say "a perfect candidate." There's no such thing as a perfect start-up for investment or, for that matter, a perfect anything else. (Except, of course, for my wife and my children, if you will allow me that highly-prejudiced opinion.) If it were perfect, then it would not be a start-up. It would be a mature company, and even then, I repeat, nothing is ever really perfect.

Any company, from start-up to multinational industry leader, can always do better. If they don't, the market passes them by, just as the smartphone market passed Intel by while Intel was plodding along under their false assumptions.

As early-stage investors, our goal remains to *maximize the probability of success*, which means reducing the risk that the start-up will fail and increasing the chances it will make a meaningful exit within a reasonable time frame. We look for start-ups that have the right **TNTBT**:

Team

A good start-up should have a winning team leading it. This is, by-far, the most important predictor of success. Many start-ups are founded with a certain idea that targets a certain market...and then things change. The market can change, the competitive landscape can change, the product can change, the business model can change—you name it, it can go sideways. If you have a winning team, they will see what's on the horizon, recognize the need for change, and adapt accordingly. Winning management teams generally have a specific look:

Size
Typically, two or three co-founders works best; however, there are exceptions. In exceedingly rare cases, a start-up can succeed with a single founder. Having too many co-founders can be problematic as well, the old "too many cooks in the kitchen" concept.

Function
A leadership team should be diversified with complementary skills and experience—that is, a business

co-founder, a technology co-founder, and an operational co-founder, one of whom is also the *visionary* co-founder. These co-founders need the right combination of skill sets and experience required for the specific start-up they're leading.

Attitude

Co-founders, and especially the CEO, need a balanced character. On the one hand, they need to be assertive and self-confident while on the other hand, they need to be willing to listen and learn from others. The CEO is the key person needing this well-rounded personality. He or she should be a leader who is entrepreneurial and resourceful, with the ability to establish trusting relationships. Furthermore, he or she needs to be able to develop a vision of the future, articulate it clearly, and convince others to follow it. We look for people who can think differently, with the ability to see the big picture, and, at the same time, have the attention to details required for success. We want people with their head high in the sky and their feet solidly on the ground. At the same time, a "my way or the highway" CEO is a disaster waiting to happen. The CEO must be able to defer to others in their areas of expertise and humbly accept advice or good ideas, regardless of where they originate.

Experience

In most cases, start-ups need a team of co-founders who have experience in the relevant field and worked in other start-ups or corporations in the ecosystem where the start-up will play.

Excellence

Generally, we want team members with numerous successes on their resumes. However, this is not an absolute. People usually learn more from their failures than from their successes, just as I did with MaxPO. They should have a few success stories, like projects they've led, deals they've closed, technologies they've developed, ventures they've founded, or something similar. Even so, if the co-founders are young and don't have a long record in business or technology, we look for signs of excellence in other areas of life, Sports championships or successful nonprofit, military, or government service can be achievements demonstrating their character, sense of endurance, grit, and skills.

Bond

Finally, the team should know each other, should've worked together or served in the military together for several years before founding the start-up. Why is this important? Because the only thing you know for sure when you run a start-up is that it will be difficult, rough, and full of tension. A team with a long history together, who've experienced success and failure together, where team members know how other members think, is a team that will stick together, help each other when the waves are high, and work most smoothly together without personality clashes.

Need

First, a start-up should define and understand the needs and/or aspirations of their users and customers; in other words, *the value proposition*. What market problem are they addressing? What value do they bring to the different stakeholders in the target market? A good definition of the problem is, many times, a significant part of the solution. Sometimes start-ups have a unique technology that doesn't solve a real-life problem. We generally avoid those. They might be good for academic projects and generate many research papers, but they don't maximize value for shareholders in a reasonable time frame.

When we analyze the need or problem the start-up is addressing, we also look at the timing of the start-up. If the need or problem already exists as a major difficulty, there can be many solutions already out there trying to solve it. This is what people call a *red ocean* with fierce competition. We look for start-ups that are addressing a *growing* need, a problem that exists today on a small scale and is expected to become a big problem in the near future. A first-rate start-up candidate also provides significant value on some well-defined metric. For example, it may reduce the time or cost required to achieve some functionality, provide new functionality not presently in the market, reduce the expertise required to achieve functionality (i.e., it's more "user friendly"), improve the user's well-being and quality of life, reduce energy consumption, improve sustainability, or something like that. In short, we look for a business that's ahead of the curve, helping solve a big problem.

Technology

An innovative high-tech start-up should have *deep technology*—technology that can deliver significant value and be the source of a *sustainable strategic advantage* for the start-up. This is the unique difference between this start-up and its competitors, the *big idea* that enables this company to win and leave competitors behind, both in the short term and the long term. I mentioned patents in Chapter 7. This is where their value really comes into play. Technology, trade secrets (new processes, for example), and/or tech based on the unique know-how of the start-up can be patented and, thereby, are protected by law. Regarding patents, I remind you that start-ups should file for patent protection before taking their solution to customers, partners, or investors.

Compared to the broader ecosystem, deep tech start-ups more frequently secure follow-on VC funding and, therefore, have lower risk and higher potential return.[20] Some start-ups might have a sustainable strategic advantage that isn't rooted in deep tech, but in some other non-tech, innovative approach such as a new business model or marketing model. These, however, are more difficult to identify in the early stages of their operation, and so we try to avoid them.

Business

The economic aspects are critical for a start-up to be a first-rate investment candidate. This includes several things:

Business Potential
Start-ups can't simply create value; they must also capture that value. This means that someone—consumers, corporations, governments, militaries—will be willing to

---

[20] Jacob Tasto, "The DeepTech Deal Funnel, Part 1: A Look at Venture Capital Funding," Different Funds (Different Funds, July 13, 2020), https://differentfunds.com/research/deeptech-deal-funnel-part-1/.

pay for using the solution the start-up provides, and pay for it on a large scale! It should, typically, be large enough that the total addressable market (TAM) will be least $1 billion.

Business Model
Start-ups need to figure out how it gets paid for the products or services it offers, and most importantly, who is the payer. It's better to have a recurring revenue business model or at least a business model with remarkably high profit margins. The business model might be different in the short term and in the long term. The start-up should not make a leap that's too big and doesn't fit existing frameworks or infrastructure in their ecosystem.

Exit Potential
As investors in high-growth, private start-ups, we look to partner with start-ups that have a potential for acquisition by a large corporation in the relevant market segment or one that has the potential for an initial public offering (IPO) in a leading stock exchange. The founders must always remain cognizant of potential acquirers of their start-up and have a well thought out exit strategy that can be articulated to investors prior to the investment. As the late management guru Stephen Covey often said, "Begin with the end in mind."[21]

Traction

To optimize the risk/reward, we look for start-ups that have found ways to progress from a nice idea on a

---

[21] Stephen R. Covey, *7 Habits of Highly Effective People* (New York: Simon & Schuster Ltd, 1989).

napkin to at least a prototype or proof-of-concept that has been used by customers or potential customers. We talk with these early users and hear their direct feedback about the problem and how the proposed solution helped them solve it. We also discuss the start-up's attitude and the way they engage with customers and users. If the feedback shows a good product-market fit potential, it gives us confidence that they're on the right path. Although we are early stage investors, we are very conscious of the statistics—only 50 percent of start-ups that raised first-round capital then go on to successfully raise their next-round funding.[22] Sadly, many ideas that look really good on paper are not able to withstand the first touch of reality.

Many first-time entrepreneurs will look at this description of a first-rate start-up for investment and will think, "Well, I can only get there after I raise money." This approach reduces the probability of raising money and leading a start-up to a successful exit.

I repeat the opinion of Reid Hoffman, LinkedIn founder, who said, "Starting a company is like throwing yourself off the cliff and assembling an airplane on the way down."

Successful start-up founders are passionate, resourceful, and innovative, and they have true grit. They can solve complex problems and make the impossible possible. At NextLeap Ventures, we look for those entrepreneurs, partner with them, and help them build a successful company. When it works, everybody

---

[22] CB Insights, "Venture Capital Funnel Shows Odds of Becoming a Unicorn Are about 1%," CB Insights (CB Insights, September 6, 2018), https://www.cbinsights.com/research/venture-capital-funnel-2/.

wins—the customers, the entrepreneurs, the employees, and the investors.

I am always inspired and encouraged by the words of Robert Noyce, Intel co-founder and first CEO, which are prominently displayed on the wall of the entry to Intel's headquarters:

"Don't be encumbered by history. Go off and do something wonderful."

Chapter 12

Leadership

This is a much shorter chapter than it could be, and that is by design. It includes many ideas. Each of these ideas could and has had many books written about it. My point here is not to explain them fully, but simply summarize my feelings on this subject to introduce you to ideas that I hope you'll explore on your own. It's based on my experience that you've read about in this book, and ultimately, it is your responsibility to build a bridge to your own leadership, success, and happiness.

Bridges to Leadership

I chose this to be the name of this book since these three words encompass the essence of my career and the best advice I can offer to people who want to develop their career, enjoy life, and have a positive impact on the world and humanity. It's all about building bridges to leadership. This is what I've been doing and what I plan to continue to do, and as you read through this book, I hope that you are also urged to do the same.

Thirty-three years ago, I graduated from the Technion, Israel's MIT, with a bachelor of science in electrical engineering and began my professional career. Since then, I have earned additional academic degrees—a

213

master's of science in electrical engineering and a master's of business administration. I served in the navy, worked at three start-ups, then at Intel, and, most recently, co-founded (with a few friends) NextLeap Ventures, an investment group of current and former Intel executives. I've also volunteered, and still do—as a founder and currently the president of the NYU Alumni Club of Israel and as chairman of the executive board for Big Brothers Big Sisters of Israel.

As I reflect on these last and very exciting thirty-plus years, I wanted to share some of my learnings about myself as a leader, my leadership philosophy, and how I see the future evolving for me and all of us.

While I believe in and practice role modeling, I enable others to act as well. I treat all people with dignity and respect, and I continuously develop and foster collaborative relationships—that is, I build bridges. Throughout my career, and as I've described to you in this book, I've built bridges between technology and business, between the present and the future, between the desired and the feasible, and most importantly, between people—different types of people. I connect people from different cultures, different disciplines, and different backgrounds.

Building bridges and connections between people allows us to reach our goals and realize our dreams. I am a strong proponent of communication, and I believe in openness, integrity and honesty when it comes to working with or doing business with others.

V.E.S.P.A.

Many years ago, I realized that leadership is the key to success. We are all leaders, and we should continue to think and behave like the leaders we already are. Let me share with you the blueprint of my leadership philosophy. I call it V.E.S.P.A[23]:

- ❖ **V**ision
- ❖ **E**mpowerment
- ❖ **S**trategy
- ❖ **P**eople
- ❖ **A**ction

Vision

This is really where it all starts. This is a compelling picture of what the world looks like when we win. It is about where we want to go and what we want to accomplish. We can paint the vision for ourselves, for our families and friends, for the organizations and societies we belong to, and for the world at large. As the Dalai Lama supposedly said,

"In order to carry a positive action, we must develop a positive vision."[24]

Empowerment

Empowerment is critical to any group of people. Delegating authority to act gives people a sense of ownership over their part of your project. With ownership comes both responsibility and a sense of personal achievement that doesn't happen when your people are just carrying out your orders.

---

[23] No relation to the Italian luxury brand of scooters manufactured by Piaggio. Although I think very highly of that brand and company, I am not involved, related or affiliated in any shape or form with that brand or that company.
[24] Attributed; frequently cited but never sourced.

Without empowerment, you can achieve good things, but not great ones. It is critical for scaling up the capabilities, and hence, the results. It is important to empower people so they can do the best they can. You want to surround yourself with people who do not ask for permission. They know what to do and when to do it, and they are not afraid of failing. As John C. Maxwell reminded us, "Sometimes you win, sometimes you learn."[25]

Strategy

Your vision tells you where you want to get to, and it is your strategy that describes how you get there. I've learned that a good strategy must be well thought out, and it must also be reviewed at regular intervals and adapted to the changing environment as you move forward toward fulfilling your vision.

As Andy Grove said, "Only the paranoid survive."[26] As Murphy said, "If anything can go wrong, it will."[27] You need to be on the lookout for surprises. Many will be sudden. Some can be far beyond any contingency you've planned to meet, but only a very small minority will be insurmountable.

By the way, in determining the *how* to deal with the future, you shouldn't reinvent the wheel every day. There are very few ideas so original that no one has done anything similar in the past. In law, this axiom is

---

[25] John C. Maxwell, *Sometimes You Win—Sometimes You Learn: Life's Greatest Lessons Are Gained from Our Losses* (New York: Center Street, 2013).

[26] Andrew S. Grove, *Only the Paranoid Survive: How to Exploit the Crisis Points That Challenge Every Company and Career* (London: HarperCollins, 1997).

[27] Dictionary.com, "Murphy's Law," Dictionary.com (Dictionary.com LLC, June 13, 2018), https://www.dictionary.com/e/slang/murphys-law/.

called *stare decisis* (in Latin, "to stand, having decided"). It means "let the decision stand" or "to stand by things decided." To put it simply, stare decisis holds that courts and judges should honor "precedent"— the decisions, rulings, and opinions from prior cases. It's the court's way of saying, "If it ain't broke, don't fix it."

We sometimes role-play. We're a VC, so we look up to the respectable and very successful VCs in the world, like Sequoia Capital and Andreessen Horowitz. They're very, very successful. They've raised billions of dollars. They've invested in hundreds or maybe thousands of companies. They've completed hundreds of exits.

When we have a tough situation, a challenge where we're unsure how to proceed, we ask, "What would Sequoia Capital do in this case? What would Andreessen Horowitz do in this case?" We try to put the hats of these people on our heads. We're different, and we know that what works for them may not work for us in whatever the situation happens to be. However, people who are really successful in what they're doing are people to watch and learn from.

"What would they do in a situation like this or that?" Almost certainly, they'd do something a little different than we'll do. But what we think they would do has proven to be a great way to start developing our own strategy.

People

We often hear about this organization or that organization doing something, right or wrong. This is a myth. Organizations don't *do* anything; the people—employees, managers, members, partners, volunteers, whoever—individuals with names, lives, and dreams do it. They carry the water or care for the needy or whatever else is necessary to take the vision from dream to reality. You don't necessarily need "the best people in the world" to change the world. You just need people committed to that vision, and they need to collaborate effectively.

We're all people—our colleagues and friends, our managers and employees, our customers, our partners, our vendors, our investors or donors, even our end-users. They're people with basic needs and aspirations. To bring them on our side and align them with our vision and strategy, we need to figure out what their needs and aspirations are and fulfill them. This way, we enrich and delight them. As Maya Angelou is often misquoted as saying, "At the end of the day, people won't remember what you said or did, they will remember how you made them feel."[28]

Action

Having a brilliant vision, creating an empowering environment, designing a winning strategy, and recruiting and nurturing the best people don't mean anything if you don't go out and do something. Taking proactive actions make a leader and an organization successful. As Joel Barker said, "Vision without action is merely a dream. Action without vision just passes the time. Vision with action can change the world."[29]

---

[28] Attributed to Ms. Angelou since 2003, the earliest known source is Richard Evans, *Richard Evans' Quote Book*. Salt Lake City: Publishers Press, 1971. Evans attributes it to a sermon by Carl Buehner, an elder of The Church of Jesus Christ of Latter-day Saints.

[29] Joel Arthur Barker, "Power of Vision," Star Thrower Distribution (Star Thrower Distribution, 1990), https://starthrower.com/products/power-of-vision-joel-barker.

Of course, this does not apply exclusively to the team members. Leading from the front is a very important mindset that I learned in the Israeli Officers Academy when I was twenty-one. This is also something deeply ingrained in Israeli culture. In many armies throughout the world, commanders remain at a command post far from the front lines. In Israel, the commanders are at the front line and often the first killed. I think many Israelis carry this idea into business.

So get out there and do it! Everything is possible if you have a V.E.S.P.A.!

Why do I choose to define my leadership philosophy as V.E.S.P.A.? Because, like the Italian scooter, it is agile and stylish—it will take you wherever you wish to go—if you are careful and mindful of the environment and people around you.

The Art of Leading People

As we're reaching the final stretch of this book, I'd like to share with you a few things I've learned about leading people. Leadership is a characteristic that is being taught in many places—school, academia, military, and the business world. However, I believe that leadership is actually a form of art and requires creativity. Some people are artists, and some are not. Some people are leaders, and some are not. Generally speaking (of course, there are always exceptions), the DNA you have and the environment you grow up in during the first twenty years of your life will determine if you are a leader or not. Later, you can and should hone your skills as a leader and fine-tune them to be the most effective as you go through your life journey. I've seen several specific characteristics, skills, and behaviors in the most effective leaders I've observed and worked with. I share them in alphabetical order, rather than suggesting that one is more important than another:

Ask Questions

A leader must be thoughtful and insightful, yet he or she must realize that no single person always sees the full picture or understands all the details better than others.

It's vital for anyone in a leadership position to consult with and get advice from experts. Asking the right people the right questions at the right time is the only way to gather the information you need to formulate a full view of your situation.

Equally, it's vital to ask those on your team what they're doing, how they're feeling, what problems they're encountering, and how they're solving them. How can you help them achieve their best work if you don't know what's going on?

Remember the words of Thomas Babington, Lord Macaulay: "Men are never so likely to settle a question rightly as when they discuss it freely."[30]

Be Friendly

Human beings are social animals. We like to interact with others. In fact, our mental health depends on it. That's why people have friends. People also need to be noticed and appreciated. Regardless of who they are or what their job is, they should be treated as an important part of the program—because they are. Every religion and

---

[30] Lord Macaulay, Thomas Babington, *Southey's Colloquies on Society.* London, 1830.

philosophy has some version of the Golden Rule: Treat others with the respect and courtesy the way you want them to treat you. In the Christian traditions, it is "Love thy neighbor as thyself"; in the Jewish tradition, it is "Love thy fellow man as thyself."

As a leader, it's especially important that you behave in a friendly manner with *everybody* around you. In a large corporation environment, there's a crew of people responsible for cleaning the facility. (Notice that specific phrasing, "a crew of people," it's intentional.) I make sure to go out of my way a little to treat them as I treat my friends—saying good morning or good evening, asking how they feel and truly listening to their replies. The same applies to the support staff. When you need a secretary or assistant to make copies, say please. If someone brings you coffee or tea, say thank you. Common courtesy is the lubricant that makes a society civil.

When you are friendly with others, you'll find that others are friendly toward you. These simple acts we learned in childhood make everybody happier, and that makes the whole workplace much more productive and effective—and profitable! It also fosters an environment where people want to help each other, because they see that their actions are appreciated. As Cicero said, "A friend is, as it were, a second self."[31]

Be Happy

Being humans, happiness should be our natural state. When we're happy, we feel better, and we operate more

---

[31] Marcus Tullius Cicero, *M. Tullius Ciceronis de Re Publica, de Legibus, Cato Maior de Senectute, Laelius de Amicitia*, ed. J. G. F. Powell (England: Oxford University Press, 2006).

effectively. Happiness is contagious to a point. People like to hang out with happy people, as it makes them feel happier. Happiness is, for the most part, a choice, and naturally follows being satisfied with our place in the world. In the immortal words of Zorba the Greek: "All that is required to feel that here and now is happiness, is a simple, frugal heart."[32]

I adopted a trick that I've used for many years: Whenever I am about to walk into a meeting, I first put on a big smile on my face. Even if I'm not very happy at that particular point in time, the smile on my face immediately makes me feel a bit happier. Most people react well to a smile. It really is contagious, and they'll smile as well. When you're happy, you are more likely to feel optimistic, and when you are optimistic, you're more likely to achieve great results. I use the smiling trick in every engagement I have—even when I come back home from work at the end of the day. Just before entering my home, I put a big smile on my face to show my wife and children how happy I am to come back home and see them.

People often express dislike for the phrase, "Fake it till you make it." Understandable, since we value honesty. However, sometimes it's the right choice. When dealing with human emotions, the actions sometimes precede the attitude. Changing the way you feel isn't like switching channels on a television or radio. There's an old story about a student and a master:

The student says to the master, "I'm discouraged. What should I do?"

The master replies, "Encourage others."

---

[32] Nikos Kazantzakis, *Zorba, the Greek* (New York: Simon & Schuster, 1946).

Connect with People on an Emotional Level

Humans are not robots. They have emotions. To get the best outcomes from people, you must "listen" to their emotions, understand them, and behave accordingly: Empathy is the ability to feel what others are feeling, or at least to recognize and understand those feelings. Sympathy is feelings or actions demonstrating compassion toward others, approving of, supporting, or showing loyalty to others. People, in good times and bad, need support and loyalty. They need to see that you are sympathetic to their cause.

As a wise dad once advised his daughter, "First of all, if you learn a simple trick, Scout, you'll get along a lot better with all kinds of folks. You never really understand a person until you consider things from his point of view... until you climb into his skin and walk around in it."[33]

In my interactions with people, I tell them about my life outside of the business world, and I ask them about theirs. I mentioned earlier that it's the nature of humanity to see the gaps that separate us and that we build bridges to close those gaps. The better we know each other, when we see and hear that our lives are more similar than they are different, then we understand each other better. We feel connections based on similar experiences, and we can communicate more effectively—and that always leads to better business results.

Embrace Diversity

Diversity is important on many levels. I'm not just talking about gender, racial, ethnic, or other minorities that have

---

[33] Harper Lee, *To Kill a Mockingbird* (Philadelphia: J. B. Lippincott & Co., 1960).

a history of forced exclusion. That's important, but it's only part of the picture.

I'm talking about across-the-board diversity in every aspect of the team. Older workers are often ignored as "behind the times," but they know what's worked and what hasn't. They can help you avoid repeating mistakes. Younger workers are often ignored as "too inexperienced to have an opinion," but they're more likely to think outside the box. They're somewhat naturally innovative. Asian and African cultures differ from European and American cultures in their ways of thinking and their worldview. One never knows where a good idea is going to appear.

Research shows that diversified groups achieve better results, not just in the business world, but also in the nonprofit world and all other social engagements:

"Infinite diversity in infinite combinations... It represents a Vulcan belief (also [Gene] Roddenberry's belief) that beauty, growth, progress—all result from the union of the unlike."[34]

As best you are able, always be part of diversified teams and partnerships, and when the choice is yours, draw your talent from every color of every spectrum.

Give Feedback

We discussed this extensively in Chapter 8 as part of the evaluation process. "Performance measured is performance improved," says an old business rule. When done in a smart way, feedback inspires people to lengthen their stride, extend their reach, and be their best. As a

---

[34] Herbert F. Solow and Robert H. Justman, *Inside Star Trek : The Real Story* (New York: Pocket Books, 1996).

leader, you're helping others build bridges and cross them, from where they are today to where they can be in the future as a better version of themselves.

Criticism has sadly become a word solidly attached to negative commentary. *Critique* is coming to mean professional-quality feedback that gives equal time to praise for good work done (which should always come first in a business setting and probably every other as well) and discussion on how to improve areas that need it. That improvement may need to be a formal plan including methods, KPIs, and dates so both parties know exactly what's expected of each. Sometimes additional training is needed, or mentoring is advisable; those as well should be part of the plan.

Finally, it is never wrong to give credit publicly or to reward achievement openly while critique should always be conveyed privately. Persons outside the problem should be involved only when absolutely necessary.

Have Integrity

Abraham Lincoln famously said: "It is true that you may fool all the people some of the time; you can even fool some of the people all the time; but you can't fool all of the people all the time."[35]

Other words that could be used in place of *integrity* include *forthright, honest, honorable, incorruptible, principled, pure-hearted, righteous, sincere, straightforward,* or *virtuous.*

---

[35] Alexander Kelly McClure, *Lincoln's Yarns and Stories: A Complete Collection of the Funny and Witty Anecdotes That Made Lincoln Famous as America's Greatest Story Teller* (Philadelphia: The John C. Winston Co., 1901).

Do your people trust you? Do you have a reputation your people respect and want to emulate? Do you have a set of guiding principles that you cannot violate? James Russell Lowell reminds us, "It is by presence of mind in untried emergencies that the native metal of a man is tested."[36]

We all make mistakes, and forgiveness needs to happen at times, but a leader must stand on solid ground. They cannot have two sets of rules. They cannot demand what they will not give. They cannot forbid a team to do something they do themselves. Every architect and builder understands structural integrity. Without it, buildings (and bridges) fall down. People fall too, and sometimes much faster and farther than buildings (and bridges). Once lost, a reputation can be the hardest thing in life to find again.

Know Your People

Don't be a stranger. Many people like to keep their business and social lives completely separate. That's understandable. Some aspects of your business and your private life need to stay separate. However, there's a lot you can appropriately share with people—your educational experiences, basic family info, hobbies— and they will naturally do the same.

Getting to know people on a social level allows you to become more connected to them. Interacting with them outside the office or shop allows others to see that you're more than just an engineer or venture capitalist, that you're also a well-rounded person with a full life. For

---

[36] James Russell Lowell, *Abraham Lincoln*, 1864.

lack of a better term, you're more "real." You'll generally feel more comfortable dealing with "real" people, and you'll do more things faster and better.

Remember, "Strangers are just family you have yet to come to know."[37]

NextLeap Ventures has a tradition: Once or twice a year, we have a social gathering for all the NextLeap Ventures partners and all the CEOs of all our portfolio companies. It's typically a dinner event, sometimes held at my home, where people just get to know each other. Many times, they find that they can help each other with good advice or a connection to a good resource, partner, customer, or investor.

Listen Intently

Hearing and listening are very different activities. Words convey thoughts, but tone, facial expressions, and all kinds of other body language cues can tell you as much or more than the words. You must listen intently, fully focused on the other person, to comprehend both the thoughts and the feelings of the person or people you talk to.

It's an old problem—it even plagued King Henry V of England. According to Shakespeare, "It is the disease of not listening, the malady of not marking, that I am troubled withal."[38] (*Withal* is short for *with it all*.)

While someone else is speaking, don't be thinking about what you'll say in response. You don't have a timer in the background. You can listen with your full attention

---

[37] Mitch Albom, The Five People You Meet in Heaven. New York: Hyperion Books (now Hachette Books), 2003.
[38] William Shakespeare, *King Henry V Part II*, Act I, scene ii, 1598.

and then think about what you're going to say before you speak—aloud and not just to yourself.

When you listen, you must absorb what you hear, see, and feel to get the full meaning of the other person's message. Internalize that message, incorporate it into your thinking, and ultimately, your decisions and actions.

Role Model

As the leader, you don't have to be the best engineer or the best salesperson or the best accountant, but you do have to be a role model in everything you say and do. The DNA of an organization is many times a reflection of the first leader of the organization. As a French moralist remarked, "Nothing is so contagious as example; and we never do any great good or evil which does not produce its like."[39]

Almost every trade or profession has *best practices*. Know them. Practice them. Exemplify them in your conduct and work. Teach those you lead what's expected of them and insist all your people measure up to the highest standards of their industry. If certifications or licensing is required, keep them current and make sure your people stay current. If rules and regulations apply, make sure to follow them, and ensure your people do the same. Don't cut corners. If you do, you shouldn't be surprised if your people do it as well.

---

[39] François VI, Duc de La Rochefoucauld, Prince de Marcillac, *Reflections; or Sentences and Moral Maxims*. Translated by J. W. Willis Bund. London: Simpson Low, Son, and Marston, 1871.

Self-Confidence

A leader must be decisive. People will follow you if they feel you know where you're going and why you're going there. This doesn't mean you should think you have all the answers or that no one else's opinion matters. Your self-confidence should include confidence enough to hear opposing views, weigh them carefully, then admit publicly when someone else has a better idea or plan or just another option that could be tried. Do bold things to achieve great outcomes for your people and with your people:

"There are times when the utmost daring is the height of wisdom... Timidity is the root of prudence in the majority of men... Boldness governed by superior intellect is the mark of a hero."[40]

Stay Calm

Behaviors and emotions work like a mirror. When you are calm, others around you will be calm. People feel safer when the leader is calm, and they operate more effectively. Anger, frustration, impatience, even disgust, are normal human emotions. They're a valuable part of our self-defense mechanism—responses to perceived threats or serious situations. That doesn't mean you should always display them publicly.

Feeling anger or other negative emotions generally happens whether you want them to or not. They can arise suddenly, in response to ridiculously small problems. They are, in the words of an old warning, like fire: "A good

---

[40] Phillip Gottfried von Clausewitz, *On War*, Books 2 & 3. Berlin, Ferdinand Dummler, 1982.

servant but a dangerous master." People who let their emotions run wild make bad decisions and say things they'll regret. Sometimes they even cross a line from which there is no going back.

You never have to be controlled by your emotions; you must always control them. There's nothing wrong, even, with letting your people see you're angry or frustrated—life is sometimes infuriating. But lashing out at people even if they're the cause of the problem is always the wrong response. Letting your people see that you're frustrated but keeping your temper in check, keeping your voice under control, dealing with whatever the problem is in a coolheaded, professional manner will always win you respect.

Watch Carefully

To form a vision, a strategy, and an action plan, you must first watch what is going on around you. "Educated men," said Aristotle, "are as much superior to uneducated men as the living are to the dead."[41] The more details you see, the more insights you can derive from a situation, and the better your decisions will be. You don't have to be Sherlock Holmes and notice every minute detail, but keeping your eyes open can bring you a wealth of data that'll make your behavior more effective moving forward.

That information, by the way, can come from many sources. Read the news to know what's happening in the world. Read trade publications and scientific journals

---

[41] Diogenes Laertius. *Lives of Eminent Philosophers*, Vol. I: Book 5. Translated by R. D. Hicks. Loeb Classical Library 184. Cambridge, MA: Harvard University Press, 1925.

to see what's on the horizon. Attend conventions and conferences to get the viewpoints of others in the industry. Investing time and effort in watching what's happening around you—and sharing the information with your people—is core to a leader's responsibility.

In addition, keep your eyes on the people around you. In every engagement, discussion, and relationship that you have, always look for new connections, bridges, opportunities, and things that you can do with someone else. It's what some people call *serendipity*, and things like that do happen, but if you don't look out for them, they will not happen to you.

Be anxiously engaged and proactive. Take the leap and say, "Yes, we'll try it. Let's do something," pushing the boundaries. Many times, these are opportunities that, on the face of things, just don't cut it. That is, if you look at them in a way that's too concrete, you'll miss out because you're saying, "This will never happen."

Open yourself to opportunities, absorb and look at what's happening around you, and try to identify the places where you can dig in a little bit more, and maybe you'll find an opportunity. Maybe you'll find a bridge to the next place that you want to get to.

Words Before
We Part

When you're done with this book, I hope you'll get a new perspective on how the world works. With these new eyes, you will, I hope, start to see bridges everywhere. And they are everywhere. That's one of the really cool things about life.

I also hope you've realized that it's your job—whatever your specific job title might be—to build bridges. It isn't just the person in charge of the project or the venture; anyone can (and everyone should) take the initiative and build a bridge wherever you can. I cannot stress enough the idea that building bridges makes every job easier today and makes more opportunities possible for you and your team tomorrow.

I am not done yet, as Robert Frost concludes in his famous poem:

> I have promises to keep,
> And miles to go before I sleep,
> And miles to go before I sleep.[42]

---

[42] Robert Frost, "Stopping by Woods on a Snowy Evening," New Hampshire. New York City: Henry Holt, 1923. Read the complete poem on several websites, including: https://stuff.mit.edu/people/dpolicar/writing/poetry/poems/stoppingByTheWoods.html.

I have many more dreams and things I'd like to accomplish. I have a lot of things I have to learn and a lot of experiences that I'd like to enjoy.

I hope that the bridge stories I've told you in this book will help you bridge between your present and your desired future.

There's one thing I'd like you to remember, more important than any other:

Life is short. It's important to be happy and enjoy the ride.

A big part of this is your family. Family is the most important value in my life. It's the family you grow up in—your dad, mom, siblings, grandparents, uncles, aunts, cousins, nieces, and nephews. And even more importantly, the family you created with your significant other—your wife, children, and grandchildren.

The family you grow up in molds you into who you are at an early age, and the family you create is your opportunity to leave a legacy and heritage. My life and career were successful so far and will continue to be successful in the future because of the strong bonds we have in our family. My parents—Chen and Raya—are my heroes and role models. They mentored and inspired me, as well as my sister, Yael, and my brother, Ron. My wife, Anat, is the capstone of the family we created together and a big source of light and support to me and our children. She is my best advisor, and she always knows how to help me overcome challenges and celebrate victories. Our children—Amit, Neta, and Edo—are my greatest pride, and I enjoy watching them become young successful adults.

Seeding, nurturing, and cultivating your family is the most important bridge you will ever develop in your life.

Always make this your highest priority. After many years and job titles, I know now that the most exalted title I have ever held or will ever hold is *husband and father*.

So what lies ahead? What will the next thirty years of my life look like? I am no fortune teller, but I do know that if I continue to dream big and practice the leadership philosophy that I shared with you in this book, then the sky is the limit. I promised myself I would keep my positive, can-do attitude, make things happen, and achieve results. I am optimistic and see a bright future for me and you.

Let us keep on enjoying the journey of life together.

About Oded Agam

Oded Agam is a high-tech investor, advisor, entrepreneur, senior executive, and strategy and innovation expert, with vast experience in a variety of fields—six years in venture capital, eleven years at Intel, and eleven years in three different start-ups. Oded is a managing partner and co-founder of NextLeap Ventures, leveraging the experience and expertise of current/former Intel executives for smart investments in early-stage start-ups. Since its inception in Q4 of 2017, NextLeap Ventures has invested in twenty-three deep-tech start-ups, had two exits in 2021 that provided nice returns to investors, and most of the portfolio companies have already had follow-on rounds with significantly higher valuations.

He is a board member and angel investor at Montfort Brain Monitor, a start-up helping to improve the quality of life and clinical outcomes for patients who suffer from neurological disorders. Oded is also a board member at HT BioImaging, a start-up that enables early diagnostics of cancer using heat diffusion measurements. Furthermore, Oded is a board observer in three other start-ups: TechsoMed, providing real time predictive visualization of true ablation damage used in interventional oncology, cardiac treatment, and pain management; Cybord, improving electronic products quality, reliability and traceability using in-line AI component inspection software; and Airwayz, enabling thousands of concurrent airborne vehicles to use the low altitude urban airspace with AI-based unmanned air traffic management system.

In his last position at Intel, Oded was a senior director leading the Strategic Technologies Group (STG) of Intel, which was part of the PEG Strategy Office (PEG was Intel's largest R&D org with more than twenty thousand engineers) and dotted line to Intel's Corporate Strategy Office (CSO). STG was chartered to identify, define, and drive new innovative technologies and IP blocks to enable sustainable strategic advantage for Intel. In this role, Oded and his team developed an annual Long-Term Outlook providing a vision of the digital world in ten years, and drove several key technologies into Intel's road maps. Leveraging both internal innovation as well as open innovation, Oded and his team drove a variety of long-lead technology domains, including computer vision, machine learning, cognitive computing, edge/fog, blockchain, wearable, augmented and virtual reality, robots and drones, and many more.

Prior to that, Oded led the definition of Skylake—sixth-generation CORE™, Intel's flagship product line for 2015, enabling revenue of more than $30 billion. In this role, Oded drove multidisciplinary teams focusing on significant evolutionary and disruptive innovations in the product line, enabling top and bottom-line growth for Intel's main line of business.

He joined Intel in 2006 as the first ATOM™ strategic planner, where he led the definition of Intel's first system-on-chip as well as numerous other products for the mobile, tablet, netbook, embedded, and IoT markets, enabling revenue of several billions of dollars.

Prior to joining Intel, Oded held several marketing, technical, and management positions in Israel and the US: VP of marketing at Discretix (later acquired by ARM),

CEO and co-Founder of MaxPO Home Networks, and VP of products for RADCOM Inc. (IPO in NASDAQ).

Oded started his professional life as a systems engineer and technical program officer in the Israeli Navy.

Oded holds an executive MBA from NYU Stern School of Business. He co-founded and serves as the president of the NYU Alumni Club of Israel, as well as the chair of the Stern Alumni Club of Israel.

Oded holds a MSEE from Tel Aviv University and BSEE (cum laude) from the Technion, Israel's Institute of Technology.

Oded volunteers as chairman of the board of the nonprofit organization Big Brothers Big Sisters of Israel.